THE TWO-DIGIT REVOLUTION

Cursive **BILL 6148 SIGNED INTO LAW: CONNECTICUT THE 22ND STATE TO REINSTATE CURSIVE INSTRUCTION, MANDATORY KINDERGARTEN TO GR 8.**
"*Enacted by the Senate and House of Representatives in General Assembly convened: Not later than January 1, 2024, the Department of Education, in collaboration with the State Education Resource Center,* **shall develop a model curriculum for grades kindergarten to grade eight***, inclusive, that may be used in whole or in part by any local [and] or regional [boards] board of education. (Substitute Senate Bill No. 1 Public Act No. 23-167 AN ACT CONCERNING TRANSPARENCY IN EDUCATION. Sec. 16. Subsections (a) and (b) of section 10-25b of the general statutes Substitute Senate Bill No. 1."* (January Session 2021 Cursive Bill 6148 was through Advocacy by Author and by 147th (Stamford) District Representative Matt Blumenthal, 2019-2023).

THE TWO-DIGIT REVOLUTION

Enhancing Writing Fluency, Reading Readiness, and Cognitive Development Through Cursive Handwriting Instruction

Celia M. Batan, BA MA CPC

Copyright 2018

Celia M. Batan, BA MA CPC

Published by TAHIKO Books

This book was published with assistance and support from The Graduate Institute Publishing Center which operates under the auspices of The Graduate Institute in Bethany, CT. The mission of The Center is to provide students and faculty with the means to create, publish, and distribute written work in both print and digital form to a world-wide audience.

To learn more: *www.learn.edu*

ISBN: 978-1-947762-04-6
Library of Congress Control Number: 2018936844

Manufactured by Thomson-Shore, Inc.

Contents

Foreword ix

Prologue xv

Summary xxiii

Introduction xxvii

Chapter One 1: The Common Core State Standards and the Vision of the Future 1

Chapter Two: Physiology and Neurology Behind Writing by Hand 7

Chapter Three: Pedagogical Considerations for Writing in Cursive 13

Chapter Four: Teaching Strategies for Penmanship and Legibility 23

Conclusions: Feasible Courses of Action 43

Works Cited 51

Appendix A 59

Appendix B 75

Appendix C 81

About Celia M. Batan, BA MA CPC 85

About Dr. James Trifone 89

Acknowledgements 93

*This work is dedicated to my mother,
the master teacher, who believes that teaching is a passion,
not a job. It means facing tomorrow with joyful anticipation
of seeing a lesson plan unfold in the light of a child's eyes.*

Foreword

The Two-Digit Revolution

Once upon a time, becoming proficient in penmanship, as well as learning to write sentences in cursive, was an important and mandated skill developed by every elementary student. Writing in cursive was not only perceived as an art form, but also as demonstrative of a proper education. Of course, those were the days when people actually wrote by hand and "snail"-mailed letters and cards for all occasions. In addition to making one's messages more personal, writing in cursive actually made handwriting more fluid and faster than printing in block letters. However, with every age come new technologies that typically result in the decrease or even abandonment of skills and practices that once were viewed as essential. Therefore, just as the horse-riding postman of the past was replaced by a fleet of trucks, trains and planes that could deliver letters and packages faster than in ages before, the rise of the Digital Age provided ways to communicate electronically even faster. In the modern world, communication technologies are continually being developed to create and share information more expeditiously.

One of the casualties of the digital age has been typing letters using a computer keyboard; or worse, texting messages on cell phones using an abridged set of esoteric shorthand symbols that make pidgin English look like a well-developed formal language. The old maxim "don't throw out the baby with the bathwater" is an apt adage to illustrate what happened when typing electronically replaced hand-writing. In this case, the art of cursive writing lost and deemed just another archaic and passé practice. However, what was unfortunately lost in this process was a natural way to foster children's creativity and critical thinking. This is the thesis of author Celia M. Batan's well-researched, insightful and paradigm-shifting new book: *The Two-Digit Revolution*. Celia was one of my most accomplished and memorable students in the Master of Arts in Learning and Thinking degree program that I coordinate for The Graduate Institute in Bethany, Connecticut.

For her Master's culminating research project, Celia chose to investigate the plausibility of including cursive writing as one of the standards in the Common Core State Standards (CCSS). As someone who grew up in an Asian culture, Celia knows the value of handwriting. High regard is placed on handwriting legibility in Asian cultures since it demonstrates character and literacy. Furthermore, what intrigued her was finding that there weren't any research studies conducted *by grade level* on the impact that writing in print, cursive, or by keyboarding has on learning and development. Nonetheless, Celia became fascinated by literature studies that claimed a "significant positive correlation between handwriting speed with legibility and students' capacity to succeed academically". This positive correlation appears to issue from the fact that the mechanics of handwriting, in contrast to typing, stimulates different brain circuits that foster creative and critical thinking.

Hence, Celia chose to defend the position that: as a means to prepare students for career and college success in the twenty-first century, Boards of Education <u>must not wait</u> 12-16 years for evidence proving the case of cursive as an efficacious practice to foster creative and critical thinking skills.

Towards this end, Celia conducted a thorough literature review on what innovative educators like Ken Robinson, Tony Wagner, and Howard Gardner have to say about skills requisite more fully preparing students to be "college and career" ready. All of the innovative educators she researched emphasize the importance of writing along with the literary skills of listening critically, speaking clearly, reading for comprehension and the value of collaborative work. Nonetheless, Celia found the CCSS was created and funded by corporate reformers with the goal to foster using electronic communication technologies. However, this initiative was not only shaped by a narrow vision of what literary skills are requisite for success in the future, but also purposefully excluded teaching cursive writing. Furthermore, she noted that the CCSS stresses a "preponderance and dominance of automation so that students must be up to speed on electronic processing".

As Celia thoroughly discusses in her book, neurobehavioral research findings have demonstrated that handwritten communication stimulates and develops brain activity in the rational-frontal lobes, visual, sensory and motor cortexes, emotional-limbic system, as well as in the corpus callosum that enhances collaboration of neural impulses between right and left brain hemispheres. Moreover, handwriting develops "the unique character of human thought, growth, and creativity".

Ultimately, the book's "take-home" message to all elementary administrators and policy makers is to persuasively argue the case that cursive writing needs to be an integral component of all elementary school curricula. The basis for this missive emerges from the explicit research findings that teaching cursive writing yields results superior to those coming from teaching keyboarding, as well as manuscript and printing writing forms, in promoting fluid intelligence and the graphomotor movements requisite to efficient spelling, syntax and text construction. Moreover, Celia's research revealed that reading text in traditional books leads to far higher levels of comprehension than does reading e-books. Most importantly, hand-writing notes led to higher levels of comprehension and "thoroughness" of recall and metacognition when compared with keyboarding notes on a laptop. Celia summarized her research findings regarding the significance of writing cursively as follows:

> "It shapes the executive functions of the brain for successful academic performance while enhancing creative and critical thinking practices required for meaningful interpretations of what we see. Even more compelling is how handwriting instruction influences neuroplasticity of the brain and contributes to character development and psychological healing".

Celia, in her new book, convincingly and compellingly expresses that educators need to deeply reflect on the findings from neurophysiology that persuasively argue for re-instating penmanship as an "art of forming letters" in early elementary classroom teaching. Only after fine penmanship is developed should learners then be taught keyboarding. Moreover, typing papers should ALWAYS follow first handwriting them. Towards this end, Celia "walked the talk" as is attested to by the fact that she hand-wrote her entire Master's research project in cursive FIRST and subsequently typed it in MS Word that was subsequently edited in pencil!!!

In closing, I highly recommend this well-researched and cogently written book to any elementary school educator interested in fostering creative and critical thinking skills amongst their students.

    —James Trifone, PhD
    The Graduate Institute
    Bethany, Connecticut

Prologue

The Curve of Things to Come

What do I mean by the *Two-Digit Revolution*? This is the term I coined to describe the growing support for a return to cursive handwriting instruction in the early years of childhood education, and for its continued use through high school.

Picture the image of the thumb and forefinger, grasping a writing implement in the essential human activity of putting thoughts to paper, forming graceful, flowing loops and curves in what we know as 'cursive handwriting'.

As a researcher of teaching strategies, I began to explore what was, for me, a burning question: Why should we care about continuing the teaching of cursive writing to young children? And should we continue to support cursive handwriting through the 12th grade and beyond?

In the digital age, as blackboards give way to smart boards and as spiral notebooks are replaced by the ambient-lit screens of mobile devices, is the long-standing tradition of writing in joined letters an outdated technology?

And finally, why are specialists in brain sciences, physiology, and education calling for a return to handwriting instruction as an essential pathway to enhancing writing fluidity, reading readiness, and cognitive development?

This book is about my discovery of how the relationship between cursive writing and brain development is better understood by weaving together research data from independent studies in neuroscience and education. The answer to the question of cursive's relevance to the future unfolds in the hidden benefits of guiding children toward engaging both the body and mind in an active form of writing. In these pages I have included, for your consideration, ways to integrate cursive writing in daily classroom activities.

Before we go any further, let me tell you a story.

A college-bound student and the parent went to a bank to set up a checking account. After completing the paperwork, the youngster was handed a pen by the bank official and was told, "Sign here."

The student looked puzzled.

"*How* do you mean, 'sign'?"

The accompanying parent was astonished to learn that a high school graduate could print the name, but did not know how to affix a signature on a document.

And was I shocked to learn that high school students in a college workforce education program could not read my board work, because I wrote in cursive!

Consider this: Unless you live in one of the first seven states that resisted the elimination of cursive handwriting instruction by the Common Core State Standards, you may live in a school district

Prologue   xvii

where this writing skill is no longer taught—and you probably were not aware that, for a long while now, it had not been required in the primary grades curriculum. In fact, just recently, an insurance agent I was speaking with was astounded to hear this, and began to understand why clients in their twenties would sign documents only in print, noting that letter formations were poor; for example, lower case **r** was indistinguishable from lower case **n**.

I began to wonder about the implications of a population that cannot read nor connect alpha characters to form a word. Does the absence of this skill directly correlate to the student's lack of fluidity in letter formations when writing down thoughts by hand? What are the implications for preparing today's children with capabilities to meet challenges of the twenty-first century economies?

If you are from a generation in which beautiful penmanship was correlated to one's character and bearing, you probably feel that cursive writing is an *art* that should not be lost, even while we become proficient with keyboard operations.

If you are of a younger generation and was entertained with a keyboard that interfaced with electronic toys, you would probably not see the point of using the seemingly slower mode of text production with paper and pen, especially when word search is a keystroke away.

And if you had chosen a career as an educator and are in your first years of classroom instruction, you are most likely writing in print form, not joining letters. And so do your students. Your classroom's chalk-and-blackboard system has probably been replaced by a computer-interfaced wall screen.

Even while there is emphasis in elementary curricula on keyboarding functions but not on penmanship, questions remain for Reading and Language Arts teachers. For example, you might ask:

How does a word processing feature such as "spell check" affect a child's *letter-word recognition* and *sequencing skills* for spelling independently?

Is the inordinate amount of time spent by the student doing homework due to lack of *fluidity in writing?*

For the teacher, what is the cost of lingering over a student essay or item test response because of the student's illegible penmanship?

What does it mean when your student is unable to compose just because a laptop is not on hand?

Is the horizon of knowledge narrower when historical documents handwritten in cursive are not readable by the student because letter formations are no longer decipherable to them?

If the question of what is lost when the pen is replaced by the keyboard has crossed your mind even slightly, my work is an invitation to you--the educator and parent--to explore cursive writing's significance to the educational and cognitive development of our most precious resource: today's children.

Those attending kindergarten in the 2017-2018 academic year will join the labor force of the year 2033. What kind of mindset will they have as they face both work and life challenges? What role does the ability to write by hand play in "career readiness"?

To my surprise, my research on the benefits of cursive writing led me *beyond* the beauty and legibility of penmanship. My exploration led me to studies in neuroscience and education, showing how the hand and the brain are intimately connected in the tactile act of writing by hand.

Elementary school teachers are directly involved in the earliest steps toward reading and literacy. When they realize that the mere formation of loops to connect lines within a prescribed space causes the child's brain activity to spring to action in unique ways, they begin to appreciate what pencil-on-paper remains to offer early learners.

Prologue

Our brains respond differently to modes of producing text. Dr. Karin James of Indiana University's Department of Psychological and Brain Sciences presented this fact to the State Legislature: forming letters on paper with pen or pencil recruits brain activity, while watching a letter appear on the screen does not. You would probably agree, too, that when you write by hand, you readily remember what you wrote as well as the space within which you had written it, and how your words appeared visually on that piece of paper.

Writing down a paraphrase is a radically different experience from typing verbatim what you hear as someone speaks: studies show you do not remember as much as when you *write your summary by hand*. These differences have far-reaching implications when developing *writing fluency* to keep up with thoughts, especially when taking notes during a lecture.

My strategy in this study of cursive and brain development was to cull all available information about the act of writing by hand. I began with the null hypothesis that cursive writing did not matter. For eighteen months, while completing my Master of Arts degree in Learning and Thinking, I considered all possible perspectives revealed in required academic readings, correlated published research studies, and continuously gathered various opinions and supporting data from informal interviews across professions.

The most challenging, yet exciting, part of my research was the task of organizing unearthed information, not to merely pigeonhole, but to shine a light on a basic human skill that advance human development: the continued use of the manual mode of letter formations for alphanumeric literacy and recording of ideas, specifically produced in cursive style of handwriting, that keeps the brain "working out".

It made sense to lead my findings toward a Position Paper, with an attempt to rephrase CCSS's K-12 curriculum goals "for career readiness" that Tony Wagner aptly defines as being able to develop creative solutions "for more difficult problems" of twenty-first century economies.

What about my null hypothesis? *Yes, cursive matters.* A lot. It shapes the executive functions of the brain for successful academic performance while enhancing creative and critical thinking practices required for meaningful interpretations of what we see. Even more compelling is the realization that handwriting instruction influences neuroplasticity of the brain and contributes to character development and psychological healing. The Waldorf Schools of North America's reading/writing program and the MindUp program first launched in British Columbia for elementary schools have long heeded conclusions that the brain can be trained to develop self-regulation and discipline.

I hope to unfold the story of the pen and the brain with words from scientists as well as educators and student populations from several parts of the world, including Europe and Asia. You will find handwriting samples in Appendix A.

I hope that you will find this examination of the physiology and neurology behind the seemingly simple act of writing by hand as fascinating as I have.

I hope that you will find practical uses for the pedagogical considerations I offer in teaching formations of "letters that join", with a call from educational psychologist Dr. Virginia Berninger for policy on modified instructions for those who are traditionally left behind. See Appendix B for ideas from teachers who recently attended my lecture presentation.

But, most of all, I hope that my research will provide the inspiration, concepts, and methods which will allow you to start your own Two-Digit Revolution, bringing the benefits of cursive

Prologue

handwriting to a generation of students whose educational development is dependent on your guiding hand.

Why am I so passionate about sharing what I have learned about cursive as a learning tool for brain development and academic success? For me, the best answer comes from the German writer Johann Wolfgang von Goethe:

> 'Knowing is not enough, we must apply.
>
> Willing is not enough; we must do."

If you are willing, turn the page and let's begin.

—Celia M. Batan, BA MA CPC

Summary

Research and Position Paper written for the program, Master of Arts in Learning and Thinking, 2015.

It seems that in the past decade, standards for legibility in penmanship and the use of the cursive style of writing have seen a decline in attention and in perceived educational value. It is surprising, therefore, that among issues that have arisen out of the installation of the Common Core State Standards (CCSS), the exclusion of cursive writing in any of the strands of standards in the Language Arts has generated numerous commentaries and studies, albeit limited, correlating brain activity and the act of forming letters by hand.

Publications have underscored today's approaches to literacy that do not appear to relate the role of writing by hand *to* success in reading and spelling, and *therefore* on meeting CCSS goals. Yet a number of studies see a significant positive correlation between handwriting speed <u>with</u> legibility and the student's capacity to succeed academically.

An examination of available publications indicates that writing by hand indeed incites brain activity for creative and critical thinking, where pressing keys to produce the alphabet forms does not. A tentative conclusion then would be while keyboarding is currently the technology that seems to be the medium for transmitting text, it should <u>not</u> be regarded to *replace* the function of writing by hand. Penning one's thoughts goes beyond drawing letters on paper to form words.

Neuroscience and Education agree that the teacher's goal is to teach the child <u>how to read.</u> To meet CCSS standards for literacy skills is to develop <u>fluency in writing</u>: letter recognition, formation, comprehension of text, and speed in joining letters for note-taking and expressive writing. However, writing fluency is undermined by lack of appropriate instruction on cursive writing, affecting time spent in completing homework and written tests. It is a general posture that manuscript learning is a prerequisite to joining letter forms to write in cursive, hence kindergarteners and first graders do not see cursive until the third grade. Two studies find that only one writing style should be taught beginning in the first grade and that cursive gets the nod. (It is interesting, however, how the *partly* discontinuous nature of the Vimala Alphabet implemented at Waldorf Schools eliminates the "print-to-cursive", "teach print only", and "teach cursive only" debate.) Dr. Virginia Berninger reframes the debate about which style to teach first by demonstrating how a child must develop all three skills by the third grade: manuscript writing, cursive writing, keyboarding.

This author agrees with findings that more comparative studies must commence now, to examine the effect of writing styles and of keyboarding to CCSS's academic outcomes for each level K-12.

It is this author's position that to prepare students for the twenty-first century, the Board of Education must <u>not</u> wait for 12-16 years for evidence proving the case of cursive.

Summary

Rather, today's educator must:

1. Take a second look at what neuroscience and physiology have to say about writing by hand and brain processes for learning and development;

2. Decide that legible, orderly, and perhaps beautiful penmanship matter. Express valuing for legible penmanship in both manuscript and cursive styles;

3. Incorporate cursive writing in all subjects including STEM, in varied and interesting ways, and as an art form

4. Use writing in cursive to help students process a learning activity or unsettling events in and outside the classroom;

5. Encourage children at K-12 levels to take notes by hand, possibly using a Mind Map structure, and encourage children at grades 4-12 to <u>compose first by hand</u>, then utilize the efficiency of word processing software for putting together the first draft, edit text, and to produce final copy for publication;

6. Motivate orderly penmanship by double-grading handwritten work: one for content, one for legibility;

7. Formally refresh teachers' cursive writing skills to model for students' penmanship with board work;

8. Involve parents in collaborative efforts to encourage legible penmanship in note-taking and submitted homework;

9. Move to develop policy and hand-writing curriculum for students with underdeveloped motor and perceptual skills.

Technology is slightly a step ahead of the debate. Possibly innovators have considered findings of the relationships among the hand, the brain, and creative work. One can now take notes about an interview or a presentation on prescribed paper and have the ability to simultaneously record with the same pen the audio of the lecture; to recall the manner in which something was actually said, all you have to do is touch with the pen tip the keyword that you've written about it and the pen plays back that segment. This writer used *livescribe*™ pen to Mind-map notes of all interviews conducted for this project, and could at any time file away the document in cloud storage.

Terms Used:

penmanship: appearance of handwritten text; handwriting

handwriting: penmanship; can appear in manuscript or cursive style

hand-writing: writing by hand

manuscript style: printing letters

cursive style: joining letters; continuous writing of letters to form a word

partly discontinuous: writing in cursive with some letters not joined; characteristic of the Vimala Alphabet

keyboarding: typing; pressing keys on computer keyboard to automatically produce letters

writing by hand: scratching paper with a writing implement and ink or graphite to draw letter forms

hand-writer: a person who writes by hand

Introduction

Consider, for a moment, this classroom scenario: in a college business writing course, a diagnostic exercise commences with a draw of topics out of a bag of Fortune Cookie slips. The task is to rapidly pen on paper, within twenty minutes, one's reflections on the Fortune Cookie message. Of five students, only one is American-born and is a new graduate, while the rest is a group of Europeans between the ages of forty to fifty plus for whom English is a second language. While the four foreigners are scratching away in cursive, the American appears uneasy. When asked why he is not composing, he says with some embarrassment, "I don't have my computer." The student doesn't go beyond three sentences.

In a class of high school dropouts, ages 19-25, attending a service skills program underwritten by the Department of Labor, one participant complains that while he can see clearly, he cannot tell what is written on the board. *Board work* is in cursive.

A most recent trip to the local bakery highlights the state of affairs for cursive writing with today's 'high schoolers'. The 16-year old attendant and the young kitchen staff could not produce the order: "write letters 'G' and 'N' in cursive and in upper case". After a couple of back-and-forths, the attendant presented two letters not only in manuscript but also with an illegible 'G' looking more like a letter 'A'.

How must today's educator view these scenarios? Should we ask: Is our educational system successfully graduating a generation of what Samuel Miller [1], a retired public school teacher and author, refers to as students with *'arrested writing development'?*

There are quite a number of commentaries and (limited) action research on the significance of cursive writing skills in the development of the brain's executive functions. However, there is virtually no study done at <u>each</u> grade level on the difference in optimal learning that writing modes make—between writing in print, in cursive, or by using a computer to generate original text.

With the exclusion of penmanship instruction by the Common Core State Standards (CCSS), the case for cursive is parsed and placed in the public forum for re-examination, especially by the seven states that have initially opted out of CCSS [20]. In fact, the Indiana Senate Committee heard a presentation by neuroscientist Dr. Karin Harman James [2] on the difference that manuscript, cursive, and keyboarding have on learning. On the table was Senate Bill 83, requiring "public school corporations to include cursive handwriting instruction in their school curricula."

The debate on the relevance of cursive writing has expanded to whether or not training should begin in grade 1, [3] and which should be taught first—manuscript or cursive, [4] and how teaching all three modes—manuscript, cursive, and keyboarding—at the appropriate grade levels is borne by research [5]. Two significant notes that have not had much press are: 1) the seemingly increasing number of teachers who do not have training in teaching cursive writing [40] (only 12 per cent with formal training, according to a 2008 survey [6]) or who may not use it at all, especially with board work, so that the children do not see the teacher form cursive letters; and 2) the consideration for instructional needs of linguistically diverse population in the classroom, [7,40] left-handed writers [7], and of those with motor skills difficulty [1,40].

My recent fascination with the whisperings and uproar on writing by hand comes from an old world perspective on what one's penmanship signifies. Asian cultures and educational systems within them value appearance and legibility in the handwritten word, for it is believed to be part of one's character and literacy that is on display. This is best demonstrated by SHODO [25], the Japanese art of writing calligraphy with a brush: "one's confidence is evident" in the brush stroke. For a progressive nation whose standards of education are viewed as a beacon for higher learning, the United States' apparent disregard for penmanship in favor of keyboarding is jaw-dropping and incomprehensible for those watching from outside the U.S., especially those whose countries are rated of lower economic stature. An on-line posting cites The Economist publication on achievement gaps, stating that The United States ranks twenty-fourth among wealthy nations in providing availability and quality early childhood education.

My intention in this endeavor is to cull information, sift through them, and arrive at an understanding of cursive writing's place in the development of a child's thinking habits and how cursive writing may help shape the child's mind perspectives [9] for future meaningful work [10,11]. Does the exercise of writing by hand, specifically in cursive, contributory to holistic education, tapping into creative and Gestalt thinking?

I hope to outline feasible courses of action to *reposition* cursive writing in classroom teaching, as an <u>integral part</u> of CCSS implementation. These courses of action shall include a consideration of comprehensive longitudinal studies of a generation of students' preparedness for college and the future, with the aim of investigating the effect of writing by hand to academic outcomes.

As of today, in the year 2015, educators are responsible for presenting a trained labor force in the year 2027.

Review of literature on teaching of cursive with today's curriculum requires reorganizing data according to the following headings:

I. The Common Core State Standards and the Vision of the Future.

II. Physiological and Neurological considerations: the connection between the hand and the brain.

III. Pedagogical considerations: Significance of writing by hand, specifically in cursive style, to child brain development.

IV. Teaching Strategies for Penmanship and Legibility: art form, music and movement, memes, creative journaling, healing, multi-lingual mastery, instruction for students with special needs.

Chapter One

The Common Core State Standards and the Vision of the Future

A perusal of the Common Core State Standards website reveals the following goal for teaching Mathematics and Language Arts: to "reflect the skills and knowledge [that] students will need to succeed in college, career, and life." [20]

What is *not* defined by CCSS is the vision of what the future stage *might look like*, so that the educator may *tie to* the future requirements of society those skill sets taught in today's classroom.

There are a number of publications that attempt to draw the picture of *Tomorrow*:

> Ken Robinson [10] sees innovative thinking, stressing the importance of play and experiential learning to prepare for an economy that would require this mind set.

Douglas Thomas and John Seeley Brown [22] see emergence of implicit learning of collaborative practices through online activities amongst participants (gaming).

Daniel Pink [21] calls for attention to right-brain activities, so that 5 aptitudes may be developed.

Howard Gardner [9] sees diversity in culture, work, as well as the procurement and processing of information. To successfully work with these, Gardner advocates cultivation of five mind perspectives characteristic of right-brain thinking.

When Gardner's five perspectives are interlaced with Daniel Pink's aptitudes [21] required for future roles in society, the following parallels become evident:

Five Minds	*with*	Aptitudes
Disciplined mind >		develop one expertise
Synthesizing mind >		find connections among seemingly unrelated sources
Creative mind >		explore new ideas and methods
Respectful mind >		work with diverse groups and ideas
Ethical mind >		work for the common good

Tony Wagner [23] (Fellow, Innovation Education, Technology and Entrepreneurship Center, Harvard) sees in a global economy creativity and innovation beyond STEM, for the U.S.A. to become a country that "produces better ideas to solve more difficult problems". Wagner has identified seven skills that must be developed in today's youth: the ability to ask the right questions (creative and critical thinking & problem solving), to collaborate across groups & exercise influential leadership, to be agile & adaptable, to take initiative & value entrepreneurship, to use effective oral & written communication, to access & analyze information, and to have a habitual application of curiosity & imagination.

Linda Hill [24] (professor, Harvard Business School), in a recent interview with Scientific American, talked about what she envisions of future business organizations based on current entrepreneurial behaviors demonstrated by innovative companies. Hill sees a transition to an economy "built on exchange of knowledge and information." In her study of creative teams and of leadership qualities, Hill reports on the following qualities that creative organizations would need to thrive: *creative abrasion* (generate ideas through debate), *creative agility* (reflection on ideas for refinement), and *creative revolution* (integrate ideas for new solutions).

These contemporary thinkers have a common projection of what the future looks like: globalization of communications, talent-sharing, rapid technological advancements, abundance of products, and aesthetic differentiation through product design. Underlying all these phenomena are the literacy skills of listening critically, speaking clearly, reading with comprehension, and writing for a global community, with a valuing for collaborative work toward social welfare.

With CCSS, however, education for the twenty-first century appears to be shaped by a myopic view of what the future brings and therefore the skills required to be successful within its framework: *there shall be the preponderance and dominance of automation so that students must be up to speed on electronic processing.* Fluency on the keyboard has heretofore begun to <u>redefine into obsolescence</u> a highly developed human skill with its highly evolved tool—the use of the hand to write down thoughts. The CCSS does not include penmanship in its 'literary strand'. It specifies in its 'Production and Distribution of Writing' the following entry:

> "Use technology, including the Internet, to produce and publish writing and to interact and collaborate with others."

Sampling interviews with parents and teachers across districts in Connecticut attest to the observance of this standard. While writing plans (e.g. outlining) might be accomplished with pen and paper, a student would be encouraged to use word processing to compose a first draft. A sixth grade teacher admitted that only if there were a shortage of keyboards would a student opt for paper and pencil. Since published product is expected in typed form, the importance of legibility in penmanship is diminished. After the third grade, a student may choose manuscript or cursive when writing by hand; if cursive is taught in elementary, it ceases after third grade. A parent reports that in her school district, cursive writing is an after-school program activity that she opted for her child, because she felt that it was a skill that reflected educational credibility.

An exception is found in one Connecticut district whose Superintendent insists that *keyboarding is purposely not taught in the primary grades*. Instead, teachers devote twenty minutes each day for instruction on manuscript writing by hand (2nd Grade Teacher, MALT, Hartford Cohort), with cursive limited to the third grade. CCSS does not look for penmanship in assessments; it is the Superintendent's *will* and *valuing* for handwriting skills that drive the instruction for proper penmanship. Twice a year student conferences with parents and faculty include showing written evidences

The Common Core State Standards and the Vision of the Future

of improvement, before and after guided practice. It is also worth noting that all teachers use the same vocabulary in teaching how to draw the letters, so that students across grade levels hear the same feedback on penmanship.

For today's student, in general, the choice to continue cursive writing depends largely on the encouragement of adults around him. A bilingual Spanish fifth grader, for example, whose parents arranged for a tutor on writing in cursive and remedial reading has developed a fascination for forming cursive letters, beaming at the realization that only he out of a class of twenty-five gets remarks of admiration from teachers on his fine penmanship. He is the only child in his class who writes in cursive. (It is not known at the time of the publication of this paper what writing style the teacher uses for board work.)

If an elementary school includes cursive instruction in the lower grades, it seems that there is no consistency in methods for teaching it. One third grade student in California, for example, brings home blank practice sheets to fill with the cursive letter for the day, without specific instructions on letter formation that the parent may support.

There is no explicit text within the CCSS website that posits cursive writing's irrelevance to its learning goals; nor is there any research cited proving that indeed it is irrelevant to twenty-first century work.

Yet it seems that the more one reads the CCSS standard in each strand for Writing and Reading, the more it appears that the act of writing by hand, especially in cursive style, is an unheralded *vehicle* for *achieving* CCSS goals.

Beginning Reading teachers know that without letters there can be no words; without proper instruction in letter formation there can be no full reading comprehension and development as a young writer; without reflective thought there can be no sustained memes that define value systems. While it is true that learning activities may take many forms, writing in cursive appears to open-up many pathways to what CCSS aims to achieve, more than the pressing of keys does to automatically produce letters.

The omission of teaching cursive to elementary school children and its zero emphasis on cursive's importance in K-12 developmental years beg the following questions:

> What could humankind lose with the demise of writing by hand?

> How is developmental learning affected by the shift *from* etching thoughts on paper *to* pressing keys for text production?

> How possible is it for the educator to take advantage of both technologies and to better shape meanings for the child in preparation for year 2027 and beyond?

> Can K-12 instruction in cursive writing and requirements for legible penmanship be an equalizer in the inequalities that, according to education historian Diane Ravitch [20.1] high stakes standards testing bring to the educational system?

It is time to look at what physiology and neuroscience say about picking up that pen, positioning it between the thumb and index finger as it rests on the middle finger, and willing thoughts to flow down the arm to gradually appear in symbolic forms with ink on paper.

─────── Chapter Two ───────

Physiology and Neurology Behind Writing by Hand

The dialogue on the wisdom of teaching children how to pen their thoughts on paper begins with the investigation of brain activity in the act of forming letters.

A study completed by Alyssa J. Kersey and Karin James, Department of Psychological and Brain Sciences at Indiana State University presents a compelling starting point. Their question was: which act recruited more brain activity, passively watching [someone else] form the letter or actively hand-forming the letter yourself? Their study showed that active training on the execution of letter formation "led to the increased recruitment of the sensori-motor network associated with letter perception as well as the insula and the claustrum, but passive observation did not." [12] The brain lit–up when the pen scratched the surface of paper to form letters, not when the eye just watched the letters formed by others.

Neurologist Frank Wilson's work on the evolution of the workings of the human hand best sets the stage for an examination of the connection among the hand, perception, and the brain. In his book, "The Hand", Wilson correlates relevant studies that explain neurologic control of hand movements. He pursued the neurobehavioral perspective:[13] "how the dynamic interactions of hand and brain are developed and reined, and how that process relates to the unique character of human thought, growth, and creativity." Here are conclusions he derived from studies: [page 97]

1. The eye and the hand "develop as sense organs through practice". (Charles Bell)

2. "the brain *teaches itself* to synthesize visual and tactile perceptions by making the hand and eye learn to work together". (Charles Bell)

3. The brain treats in the same way the most sensitive portions of the skin at the tip of the thumb and index finger and the macula, the most sensitive part of the retina. (Charles Sherrington).

4. The simplest movement of touching a dot on the screen requires a huge computational demand on the brain. (Scott Grafton, John Mazziota, Roger Woods, and Michael Phelps, UCLA) page 108

5. The two hands work together [i.e., they must be viewed as a partnership]. "In writing . . . . the non-dominant hand plays a complementary, though . . . covert, role by continuously repositioning paper in anticipation of pen movement . . . " (Yves Guiard) [page 159]

F. Wilson invites us to take a good look at what the dominant hand is doing as text is written by that hand. The collection of up and down marks are a product of 'muscle synergy' [page 162] of muscle contractions: slow (tonic) and fast (phasic). The thumb, index finger, and the middle finger attempt to maintain pressure on the pen "while at the same time moving the wrist"; in the meantime the forearm and hand muscles sustain the contraction. The brain adapts by sensory monitoring to eventually create micrometric movements that are memorized with constant practice. Connecting shapes to form words and sentences are produced with variations of controlled vertical and lateral movements. The coordination of the hand, the brain, and the eyes makes handwriting orderly and predictable.

Marc J. Seiffer, author of "Handwriting and the Structure of the Brain" offers a most succinct synopsis of the sequence of *activities in the brain* when pen scratches paper: [13.1]

1. The decision to initiate the movement is in the frontal lobes.

2. The limbic system joins in to provide emotional content.

3. The visual cortex sees the paper; visualizes letter forms.

4. The left angular gyrus of the parietal lobe "converts visual perception of letters into comprehension of words."

5. When words are spoken, Broca's (motor) and Wernicke's (sensory) areas process and comprehend those words.

6. The corpus collosum, which connects the cerebral cortex's left and right hemispheres, "combines the pictorial/holistic right-brain procedures with their sequential/linguistic left-brain counterparts."

7. The parietal lobe coordinates all these signals with the motor cortex, producing the motor signal to the arm, hand, and the fingers.

A simple illustration of the physiological-neurological connection when writing by hand is offered by MIMLearning.com:

Sensory motor activities key:

V = vestibular **P** = proprioceptive **T** = tactile **Vis** = visual **A** = auditory

Fixation and movement of eyes across paper- Vis, V, P
Holding head steadily- V,P
Clearly seeing and making sense of writing- V,P
Saying material to self- A
Holding neck still so writing is clear- V,P
Ignoring contact with chair, desk, with feet on floor- T
Arm resting on desk- T
Holding pencil –T,P
Moving fingers, hands, wrist, and arm while writing- T,P
Holding static posture in chair- V,P
Ignoring feeling
Listening for teacher, ignoring background noise- A

One interesting way to investigate the relationship of the brain with the hand when writing is to consider changes in penmanship at the onset of disease. An excellent reference is The Dana Foundation's citation of Marc J. Seiffer's report on how handwriting can indicate presence and progression of disease, due to damage of brain parts—"lobes of celebral cortex, limbic system, hippocampus, brain stem, and cerebellum—and finally the spinal cord, which sends impulses to . . . hands and fingers." [13.1]

The resulting forms in penmanship due to disruptions in 'brain communication' are "tremors, breaks within letters, involuntary movement, broken forms, and regressive or child-like styles".

Physiology and Neurology Behind Writing by Hand

When fine motor control is disrupted, as in Parkinson's disease, symptoms could include loss of movement (akinesia) and loss of postural reflexes. One's handwriting could show a dramatic reduction in letter size (micrographia).

A bullet through the brain that has cut-off part of the corpus collosum, like James Brady's during the assassination attempt of Ronald Reagan, can affect letter formations; Brady changed his "m" and "B" letter forms, hence modifying his signature.

Surgical severance of the corpus callosa to subside "electrical storms" between the brain hemispheres of those with severe epilepsy has shown cases of writing shifts between manuscript and cursive, poor spelling, erratic spacing, letter substitutions, intelligible words, and child-like writing style. Patients have also shown "unnatural stops and starts between and within letters, called arrhythmic splits."

A scrutiny of a stroke patient's handwriting two weeks before the episode, two weeks after the stroke, and ten years later has shown "letters that are sandwiched together," and "missing parts of letters and whole letters."

Words are understandable as they are read by context; nevertheless the changes in penmanship through time are unmistakable.

The bold, clear, and rhythmic handwriting of a man suffering from multiple sclerosis suggested that "lesions of his frontal lobe may not be as severe as his MRI suggests." Evidence of his disease is seen in spelling mistakes and hesitations within and between letters. Involuntary movements could be interpreted as "deep brain lesions in the callosum, pons, medulla, and cerebellum".

Progressive brain tumor on a man reflected degradation of fluidity in handwriting due to eventual "disruption of activity in his right parietal lobe", "brain damage caused by seizure", and problems from deeper areas of the brain.

Penmanship also reflects the recovery process from a coma. Problems in writing speed, steadiness, changes in pressure of pen on paper, variation in letter sizes, and misplacement of punctuation marks are attributable to problems in the lobes of the brain. A patient's overall grace in writing is affected by disruptions of signals.

Indeed, disorderly penmanship or sudden deterioration of penmanship can signify physical and/or psychological illness.

Chapter Three

Pedagogical Considerations for Writing in Cursive

In the 1960's pre-digital age of Education, efficient writing by hand was taught with cursive style in grades 1-6, with a published call by Dr. E.A. Enstrom (Director of Research and Instruction, Peterson Directed Handwriting, Greensburg, PA) to sustain the "vigor" to encourage legible cursive through high school, "to meet occupational needs" of the student. [8] Legible script meant "efficient, rapid skill that saves school time in the writing process and reader's (teacher's) time" in the grading process.

The twenty-first century descent of CCSS onto the teacher's table has brought to question the comparative value of handwriting styles to learning—manuscript or cursive—versus text production by typing on a computer.

To examine the effects of writing styles on the development of writing skills of second graders, professors of the University of Montreal (Isabelle Montesinos-Gelet), Universite de Sherbrooke

(Marie-France Morin) and Universite du Quebec a Rinouski Sherbrooke (Natalie Lavoie) [3] pursued research work suggesting that graphomotor skills are important: "to generate creative and well-structured written texts, students must master the mechanical tools of getting letters, words, and sentences onto the page at a <u>level of automaticity</u>". [14] Their year's work arrived at the following conclusions: [page 121]

   a. Children who used both manuscript and cursive styles did not perform as well in spelling.

   b. Cursive style showed improvement in word production and syntax.

   c. The higher the writing speed, the better the spelling and text performance.

   d. It is better to teach a single handwriting style to avoid dual learning.

   e. Automaticity in writing by hand must be aimed "at the beginning of the schooling, with direct and explicit teaching of letter formation".

This collaborative study of 718 second grade students and teachers in 54 second grade classrooms brought to light the dominant cause of more than 50 percent variance in the students' speed and quality writing: being taught how to print in Grade 1 then switching to cursive in the second grade adversely affected writing skills, demonstrating the least progress in spelling. "Teaching both types does not promote acquisition of automatic motor movements, which play an important role in spelling and text construction." Professor Montesinos-Gelet explains that the child's rapid growth in word acquisition is impeded by the switch in second grade from one style to another.

In the same study, speed and legibility showed improvement by the end of first grade, whatever the writing style taught (print or cursive), but spelling suffered when the writing style was switched in second grade. In contrast, not switching made motor movements automatic.

The notable conclusion of the study is that among teaching sequences (print only, cursive only, or print then cursive), "students who learned cursive benefitted the most... with better results in spelling and syntax." Cursive's feature of joining letters forced students to follow a path to form letters and eliminate writing backward letters or reversals (e.g. b vs. d) Also, writers in cursive do not show problems with spacing between words; they grasp the concept of a word more quickly, tending to have "better graphic-motor skills related to language processing." The study concluded that it is better to teach cursive in the first Grade.

The scrutiny of keyboarding consequences on learning was undertaken in 2005 by cognitive scientist Marieke Longcamp by using the unfamiliar Bengali alphabet. [15] With children, letters were recognized more readily when previously learned by hand, than by typing correctly. With adults, recall of handwritten letters was better than with typed letters. Longcamp has attributed the better recall to the neurological instructions present when pen is on paper, but are absent when pressing keys to automatically produce the letter form.

Norwegian professor Ann Mangen and French professor Jean-Luc Velay presented in a book, "Advances in Haptics" [48] their survey of research literature on writing by hand. (Note: however, it is not clear in the report what style of penmanship was used, cursive or printing.) When using an ink pen, the writer's attention is dedicated to the tip of the pen, the writer graphomotorically forms the letter, has to have conscious control of arm movement, monitor the pressure of pen tip on paper, and regulate with the non-writing hand the angle of the writing surface. In contrast, with keyboarding there is no haptic input, just a division of two distinct "spatiotemporally separated spaces: motor space (keyboard) and the visual space (screen)", with a single task: to spatially locate letters on the keyboard.

The brain has evolved to recognize forms, so that it regards letters and words not only as sounds and ideas, but also as physical objects. It recognizes a letter "by their particular arrangements of lines, curves, and hollow spaces". Karin James' study [2] showed increased brain activity of children while writing letters by hand, compared to no brain activity when they tapped the keyboard to produce the same letter. Dr. James also reports of a preliminary study demonstrating that after a week, college students remembered better information noted in cursive, compared to notes written in manuscript or entered electronically.

What is the influence of the motion of writing by hand on orthographic representations in memory? Researchers Bosse, Chaves, & Valdois [47] looked at how a whole word is acquired by building together visual and auditory forms of the word. Earlier studies have shown that reading <u>and</u> writing presents a better orthographic learning situation. The researchers then proceeded to test the hypothesis that "<u>specific movements</u> memorized when learning to write may participate in the establishment of orthographic representations in memory". Using fifth graders, they compared learning between writing by hand the spelling of a word and by spelling aloud. The study concluded that hand-writing made orthographic learning more efficient.

Interestingly, researchers Gene Ouellette and Talisa Tims [49] found that with 40 second grade participants, there was no difference in learning between those who practiced spelling by printing words versus those who practiced with a keyboard. (Note: it is <u>not</u> clear in the report that "printing" meant manuscript style.)

Since letter recognition is a prerequisite to reading, perhaps another way of looking at the significance of neurological activity to comprehension is to consider conclusions of comparative studies on reading paper books and e-reading: for extensive reading of unembellished text (no linkages to movie trails, for example), paper remains to have the advantage over screens. Test scores on comprehension are higher with respondents who turned physical pages and ended up 'knowing' than those who scrolled down a screen, and who 'merely remembered'. A summary of the observations below underscore the multi-sensory aspects of paper book reading: [16]

1. Holding the book gives the reader its discernible shape, size, and weight. E-reader displayed pages are "ephemeral", hence do not give one the sense of what is past and what's ahead.

2. To most consumers surveyed, the following mattered: (Abigail J. Sellen, Microsoft Research Cambridge in England)

..the "feel of papers and ink, option to smooth or fold a page with one's fingers," ... "the distinctive sound at page turns." (*C. Batan: How about the smell of paper and cover?*). E-readers have not been able to duplicate these aspects.

3. The eight corners of an opened book provides a 'mental landscape' with which the reader orients himself. Text on screen does not provide this topography; it does not give the sense of where one is in the book.

4. Turning pages gives the reader a sense of awareness and rhythm for the whole text. Assessing quickly where the

beginning, middle, and end are makes it less taxing cognitively (Ann Manger, University Of Stavanger, Norway. January 2013). "Knowing your progress [means] you have more capacity for comprehension". [page 51]

5. Light reflecting off ink and paper is ambient. While E-ink reflects ambient light, screen light shines directly on the face. Prolonged reading on glossy, self-illuminated screens make it more mentally taxing and physically tiring (eye strain, headaches, and blurred vision).

[A note from the author: this book in E-book format is only for purposes of immediate accessibility.]

Reading comprehension is affected not only by how information is processed, but also by <u>how it is recorded</u>. Note-taking has also been studied for not only recall of facts but also of 'knowing'. Authors and psychologists Pam A. Mueller (Princeton University) and Daniel M. Oppenheimer (University of California-Los Angeles) [42] studied "thoroughness" of recall, which was poor when the laptop was used to take lecture notes. Those who hand-wrote what they heard remembered context of key information better than those who typed *verbatim* what they heard. It was concluded that the process of summarizing, making decisions on relative importance of a fact, and the 'shorthand' symbols for representing the information generated a higher neural multisensory activity in the brain rather than the act of typing 'mindlessly'. In this case, the hand's unique relationship with the brain during composition is apparent.

A most notable publication on note-taking by hand is Tony Buzan's "the Mind Map Book". [27] It discusses how penning thoughts on paper also allows the creative representations of information with figures (stick figures, curved and straight lines, boxes). The process of mind mapping gives the significance of writing by hand a second look. Buzan's examination of the disadvantages of standard linear note-taking (that is, excessive words requiring re-reading for comprehension; poor idea associations that fail to stimulate the brain creatively) have led to the note-taking technique of jotting down key words in the same format that the brain's cortical function employs: *branching out word/idea associations from a key word*. Mind-mapping by noting only relevant words for easily discernible associations saves time: 50-90 percent in taking notes, more than 90 percent in reading keywords, and more than 90 percent reviewing the resulting map. With the brain remembering "visually stimulating, multi-colored, multi-dimensional maps" (rather than monotonous visual, boring notes), concentration and learning are enhanced. The Mind Map is in harmony with the brain's predisposition "for completion of wholeness". [pp 89-90]

As most hand-writers interviewed admit, they remember information noted earlier not only by how they penned it on paper and with which color ink, but also by location on the page and *how they felt* when they penned the thought.

Scientific American November 2013 issue [16] also reports on how reading on screens does not promote "what psychologists call metacognitive learning regulations"—setting specific goals, re-reading difficult sections, and checking how much one has understood along the way—a "knowing" (rather than remembering) which note-taking by summaries, cryptic notes, or symbols enhances. The article also cites a 2011 experiment at the Technion/Israel Institute of Technology about students who studied for an examination using pen and paper "approached the exam with a more studious attitude than their screen-reading peers."

Technology's attempts to duplicate the hand-writing-brain process with the 5" x 7" (estimate) Tablet products fall short in the dimension for hand and arm position in relation to the writing surface.

Also, there is no kinesthetic effect when writing on the screen. Formation of letter is not as good as pen on paper probably because the stylus is thin and short pressing on a small area. The non-writing hand either supports the Tablet under it or uses two fingers to hold it down firmly onto the table, which is quite different from the way it would have helped the writing hand keep the paper angled for the desired writing slant.

It seems, then that teaching cursive is an unrecognized pathway to attaining performance goals of CCSS for reading: "... *to read deep and wide... the standards... outline a progressive development of reading comprehension... to gain more from what they read.*" [20] Language Arts teachers would insist that reading is not separate from writing—in fact, print recognition is the beginning of reading. Writing crystallizes information and taps into the creativity of the child.

To write fluently means to form letters by hand without too much thought about graphology, thus freeing space to process other learning input. Along with reading comprehension, fluency in writing by hand is key to a student's success and achievement in K-12 grades. Fluency may be best achieved though cursive style of writing because connecting letters to form each word increases the speed of penning ideas. Cursive writing promotes automaticity in the act of forming letters. Historically, in fact, cursive writing in both Eastern and Western cultures evolved out of the need to pen thoughts faster. [41]

To highlight the crucial point of writing fluently, Samuel Miller [1] outlines the adverse effects of <u>not teaching</u> proper handwriting skills, specifically cursive, in children's development as writers. <u>Lack of fluency</u> in writing by hand comes from:

1. Difficulty with letter formation or recall of graphology which in turn slows down handwriting speed.

2. Concentrating on motor skills of handwriting (how letters are formed, how pencil is held, positioning of arm and of non-writing hand) "strains.... processing capacity in working memory", resulting in "less attention available for higher order skills like planning, content generation, and revisions."

3. Lack of fluency and resulting inefficient note-taking, so that the writer will not be able to keep up with thoughts.

4. Lack of fluency and speed, bringing about inefficiencies in studying: they affect how long homework is completed and they hamper the ability to take notes in class.

5. Consistent difficulties in letter production, leading to discouragement in writing and disinterest in other writing processes like planning and revising.

6. Difficulties of students with disabilities that are compounded without instruction on handwriting.

In his book, "The Story of Handwriting", [41] Alfred Fairbank quotes Robert Bridges, British poet (1844-1930): "true legibility depended upon *certainty of deciphering*"—meaning, one's penmanship must be clearly readable so that the text message is clearly understood. [p.78] Legibility with firm intention brings about ease in reading. Might grading content then be affected by legibility of penmanship? One's penmanship apparently influences the perception bias of the reader. Miller [1] mentions a 1992 research by Sweedler-Brown where 27 original essays (same version) written in 3 graphic modes were graded: typed, nicely handwritten, and poorly handwritten. The highest scores went to the nicely-handwritten version, with no difference in scores between typed and poorly written copies.

Even while there may be plans to eliminate essay writing in the

SAT, the recorded observations on student writing performance are worth noting.

A study of graded SAT essays also reveals the same bias for those written legibly. [26] With an average time of 3 minutes to read and assess an SAT essay, a rating of 1-6 points is awarded the essay. The score of zero is given an essay off the topic, non-English, not written in #2 pencil, considered *illegible after several attempts at reading*, or if left unwritten.

So while it may not be difficult to imagine a teacher's or evaluator's frustration in comprehending illegible penmanship, the extra time required to decipher written answers in tests, and the resulting "resubmits" for students, further study is required to verify the correlation between ratings for written text and its readability.

The implication on the student's development as a writer is also made evident in public examinations. Dr. Vi Supon [7] of Bloomsburg University cites in her paper published by The Journal of Instructional Psychology the finding that writing an SAT essay in cursive did not only do slightly better than any other type of writing, but the writing fluency (speed) with cursive allowed the student to write more than a page. Professor Supon picks up the quote of a trained scorer for the SATs (Los Angeles Times, 2005, p.1) saying that while length did not guarantee a higher score, "Nobody who got one of the top scores wrote one page or less."

Chapter Four

Teaching Strategies for Penmanship and Legibility

Considering the veracity of the neurological basis of writing and reading comprehension, how do we put together the suggested correlations among letter recognition, the nature of cursive writing style that mitigates problems of letter inversions and reversals, develops writing speed, and forms study habits that translate to work ethics required by the twenty-first century?

The marriage of neuroscience and education lends context for teaching mastery in the language arts and reading through focused instruction in writing cursive.

In her keynote address to teachers and policy makers at the Neuroscience and Education Symposium, Dr. Hardiman [17] underscored education's major goal: *to teach the child how to read*. Dr. Hardiman begins with "neuromyths" that teachers continue to hold, influencing the production of ill-designed learning plans, and that nurture toxic stress in a child struggling to read with 5-10 percent comprehension.

Here are what are _untrue_ about the brain and learning, and what a teacher could do instead:

1) *"children can still learn [at any point]."* They don't, after a certain age. Teach according to developmental age.

2) *"learning styles are different for boys and girls"*. Teach with a multi-modality approach: auditory, kinesthetic, and visual.

3) *"there are individual learning styles."* Design learning units that reflect a multi-sensory approach.

4) *"there is a left hemisphere and a right hemisphere" to each of which we should teach.* Teach with the view that the two hemispheres, though distinct in function, work together. Designing activities that address both allow for better comprehension, recall, and assimilation.

5) *"there is no connection between emotion and learning".* (Yet students learn from teachers they like/admire!) Teach to include goals for both cognitive and affective levels of performance.

6) *"art is of a separate learning."* Teach with the aid of performance and visual arts to develop areas in the brain connected to critical thinking and creative problem-solving.

In an attempt to connect brain research with effective teaching for the twenty-first century schools, Dr. Hardiman presents "The Brain-Targetted Teaching Model" [18] with six areas that teachers must consider, based on meta studies:

1. Emotional Climate: There is a connection between the affective and the biological states- stress impedes learning, positive emotions help learning. Anxiety tops the list of emotional states in a child, followed by boredom, enjoyment of learning, hope, pride, relief, and anger.

2. Physical Learning Environment: Surroundings should trigger attention in children due to novelty in what they see, in order and in beauty, and classroom layout that encourages movement.

3. Design of Learning Experience: Present the big picture first so that the child sees the interconnectivity among details and their relationship to the big picture. Imbed learning and memory with a variety of activities, including writing of reflections on the subject (journaling).

4. Skills, Content, and Concepts: Teach for mastery through repetition and mental rehearsal; elaborate through art integration. "Different neural processes are at work in creative and divergent thinking," Dr. Hardiman emphasizes. Visual and performing arts within the classroom heightens engagement and allows the child "to apply knowledge in creative thinking and problem solving".

5. Divergent Thinking: Allowing more open-ended questions rather than just filling-in the blanks develops the child's habit to consider multiple solutions to a single problem. With activities completed in real-world context, (e.g., applying knowledge of measuring land areas to designing a community garden), the child develops 'adaptive expertise'.

6. Evaluation of Learning—Create situations that allow the child to actively retrieve information (projects), evoke emotion through the arts, to receive frequent but spaced-out-over-time feedback, and the opportunity to self-assess.

To incorporate all six areas for reaching the goal of teaching a child *how to read* is to consider the *manner* in which cursive letter formats are taught. Putting together findings from available studies leads to the following *better practices* (for now) in teaching cursive:

- as an art form; with music, movement, and utterances;
- teaching values through cursive writing;
- journaling in cursive to synthesize information and possibly to heal and "make whole",
- teaching instead multilingual fluency with a learning sequence for manuscript, cursive, and keyboarding in K-3, with applications in K-4 to 12; and
- designing specialized instruction for teaching hand-writing to a diverse student population, for example, bilingual students with a different set of written language tradition, and children with biologically-based learning disabilities (dysgraphia, dyslexia, dyscalculia).

A. Teaching Cursive Writing as an Art Form

"Why not teach letter writing as an art form?"

This proposition coming from a four-year art teacher reflects the position of two authors—an art professor and a handwriting consultant.

Dr. Betty Edwards [28] of the California State University's Art Department sees cursive writing not as scribbling of words on paper but as a global skill (like reading and walking) that is a function of abilities of perception: of edges, negative spaces, relationships, light and shadows, and perception of the whole (Gestalt). Teaching how to write the letter 'A' is leading the child to knowing how to draw the figure called 'A'; 'art with a capital A' [p. xii]. Learning placement and strokes of the art of the alphabet characters accesses the R-mode of the brain [32], hence stirring creativity. In her book, "Drawing on the Right Side of the Brain", Dr. Edwards explains that drawing is an efficient way of gaining access to and control over functions of the right hemisphere [that] . . . "help children become adults who use the whole brain". [page 240]

Jennifer Crebbin [32], handwriting consultant, proposes that the best way to teach consonants is "in an artistic way through pictures and stories". [p. 32]

The belief that cursive letters could be taught as art could be what David Peat posits in his book, "The Blackwinged Night" [29] that humans have the predilection to be creative because they are the very expressions of the Creative Universe. Teaching letters as art, then, is in harmony with the child's nature. As a global skill, cursive writing is a skill for life, with penmanship evolving as the individual develops and as he changes his perception of the world around him.

Teaching cursive writing as art presents an opportunity to install Elliot Eisner's [30] art room into other academic subjects such as STEM, and thus infuse classes with R-brain activities. Imagine what a student accomplishes with one activity, when writing in cursive his reflections on a science experiment: cementing connections among ideas, forming valuation for the ideas, and inciting multisensory brain activity while connecting letter formations.

B. Teach Cursive Writing with Music, Movement, and Utterances of Letter Sounds

"Writing is a dance of the pen", Alfred Fairbank quips in his book, "The Story of Handwriting" [41]. Associating graphology with kinesthetic and auditory sensations aids in forming memories.

The rhythmic up and down strokes interspersed with lateral movements of fluent cursive writing develops 'kinetic melody' [13.1] that is unique to one's penmanship. With beginning writers and readers, 'feeling the shape of the letter 'O' can be initially experienced by walking its shape on the floor in the precise sequence of drawing it—or by tracing with the finger on sand paper cut in the shape of the letter. Other devices that exercise the imagination are tracing in the air the letter form, or on a partner's back, following the teacher's demonstration of strokes on the board. Author and novelist Philip Hensher [31] in his book, "The Missing Ink", footnotes of a school teacher in Virginia, Liora Laufer, who has coined the term "callirobics" for her exercise class in cursive writing set to music. Doing a series of repetitive hand movements to music aims at improving penmanship with correct letter shapes.

Music releases dopamine to the basal ganglia, which controls the initiation of movement. If practice in cursive writing is set to music, it fosters a positive valuing for learning cursive. In the article, "The Healing Power of Music" [43], William Forde Thompson and Gottfried Schlaug summarize changes in neural activity across brain regions (neuroplasticity) where emotion, reward, cognition, sensation, and movement are involved:

1. Music is physical—induces movement to rhythm and beat.
2. Music is emotional—induces positive states that in turn increases changes in the brain.
3. Music is engaging—invites to participate with focus, enthusiasm, and dedication.
4. Music permits synchronization—addresses problems of timing, initiation, and coordination.
5. Music is persuasive—believing that you can dance and that you can be successful supports a positive attitude
6. Music is social—engaging in group musical activities enhances social, language, and motor skills

Teaching with music seems reflective of Rudolf Steiner's "Eurhythm", [33] which he founded with Marie Von Sivers in the early 20th century. Mentioned by Jennifer Crebbin [32] in her book, "Soul Development through Handwriting", Eurhythm is performance art of expressive movement (used especially in Waldorf Schools) "to bring out creativity in a child—imagination, ideation, and conceptualization" and to improve "balance, coordination, ..and.. rhythm". Just as important is the heightened awareness of patterns—a "knowing" that's requisite in drawing letters. Eurhythm cultivates a feeling for the qualities of straight lines and curves, directions of movement in space, contraction and expansion, and of color. [33]

Jennifer Crebbin [32] specifically refers to Rudolf Steiner's 'Eurythmy of Visible Speech' as a framework for defining with letter sounds the affect of letter formation. Using the Vimala Alphabet developed by Dr. Vimala Rodgers [34], Crebbin proposes that vowels "are best represented and characterized through physical gesture, image, and sound of the vowel...."

C. Teach Values and Build Self-Esteem Through Cursive Handwriting

How is it possible to impart values when writing by hand?

A brief glimpse into Far East Asian writing offers a different perspective on a skill that is apparently "unnecessary" in the digital age.

At the end of last year's Yale University Summer Program for international high school students preparing for entry into The U.S. university school system, a Chinese student presented (this author) the instructor an extraordinary note of appreciation on a four-by-four gold tissue. The student's ardent message of 'thanks' was in calligraphy, each of 16 characters reaching out with its intended meaning as the reader transcribed the ideogram. She believed that it was proper and important to express appreciation for her classroom experience with her hand's brush strokes. (It was an overwhelmingly beautiful gesture.)

Chinese calligraphy has evolved into the Zen practice of Shodo [25, 25.1, 25.2], the art of using the brush to write Japanese calligraphy. In Japan, cursive style Sosho is learned by elementary school children. The study of Shodo goes beyond streaking ink on paper: the calligrapher must be in a clear state of mind (*mushin*) and let the letters flow as the mind unites with the spirit of the universe. Shodo requires concentration and fluidity in execution, as the calligrapher has only one chance "to create with the brush". It is unthinkable to correct strokes. If the writer lacked confidence at the moment of the stroke, the work makes it evident. One's calligraphy reveals the *character* of the writer: the production of the ideogram, the choice in metaphor, the flow of meanings.

There is no better way than Shodo calligraphy to demonstrate the transmission, through cursive writing, of societal values. Children are taught that the intent to show one's humble self with the brush dipped in ink onto paper is all important; to communicate clearly and eloquently with choices of symbols is to be one with the universe; to execute with a single stroke grace and accuracy is a noble deed. Author Eido Tai Shimano [25.1] defines Zen calligraphy as "the meeting place of art and enlightenment"—with appreciation of nature, beauty, serenity, and spirituality. In Japan and China, calligraphy reflects the character of the nation's culture. Hiragana, a kanji form of graceful cursive writing originally meant only for women, was developed for concise, speedy writing. In Zen calligraphy, form precedes sound and meaning. [25.1]

The calligrapher's work is so profound with its 'signifieds' that gazing at Shodo calligraphy is essential to clearing one's mind before commencing a Japanese Tea Ceremony.

In Western culture, before the advent of typed letters, penmanship was a separate, graded academic subject and was aimed to show character more than content [7]. It was also a vehicle to develop character and cement social values in children, including pride for one's quality workmanship.

Each aspect of literacy—listening, speaking, reading, and writing—is learned within the context of a value system. The brain's executive functions [50] that "form the foundation for many of the qualities and abilities necessary to succeed in school—and in later life" include goal setting, planning, execution, focus, persistence, and restraint. Research in children's cognitive development now suggest that these essential brain functions are trainable; "the environment can alter their course". A most compelling intervention in education that was a subject of multiple studies is the MindUp program launched in 2005 at the Vancouver Elementary School in Vancouver, B.C. [50] that has since spread to other countries. Conceived by actor Goldie Hawn (www.thehawnfoundation.org/mindup) in 2002 with educational psychologists, neuroscientists, and teachers, MindUp aims to develop the character of the mind, providing children with productive ways to negotiate with their environment and exercise self-regulation.

MindUp implementation in the classroom is accomplished with multi-modal instruction. Children are taught the names of parts of the brain and what they do, so that they could label how they feel in terms of brain functions: *breathing calms down my amygdala (emotional responses) to make my prefrontal cortex (executive function) so much smarter, and my hippocampus helps me remember.* In this program a teacher has a lesson on brain anatomy for each grade level, which is interspersed with goals for academic subjects, behavior modification, language development, and development of values critical to future roles in society, not unlike those espoused by H. Gardner's mind perspectives [9] and D. Pink's disciplines [21]. Inherent in the program are daily brain exercises like focusing on features of an object for recall, feeling features without sight, breathing while being aware of body parts, meditation, and _reflective writing on personal experiences_.

Even while more studies have to be conducted to prove actual measurements for the brain's executive functions, the success stories in British Columbia, Canada, U.K., and Venezuela, the US had seen an increase in interest in MindUp programs. At the time of this 2012 report on MindUp, 75 schools in the U.S. had implemented it, along with similar programs like PATHS (Promoting Alternative Thinking Strategies) created by psychologists Mark. T. Greenberg (then at U of Washington) and Carol A. Kusche (Seattle), and programs to teach executive function funded by CASEL (The Collaborative for Academic, Social, and Emotional Learning) [50].

It is not known at the writing of this position paper how the implementation of CCSS has affected the reported successes of MindUp in the US, including the Academic, Social, and Emotional Learning Act of 2011 introduced by Ohio congressman Tim Ryan, Illinois Representative Judy Biggert, and Michigan Representative Dale E. Kildee. The Act aimed to "expand the availability of programs that teach student skills such as problem-solving, conflict resolution, responsible decision-making, relationship-building, goal setting, and discipline."[50]

Indeed, the educator is a change agent in the classroom, especially when teaching writing through cursive. An extrapolation of Dr. Don Beck's SPIRAL DYNAMICS (*TGI video lecture S13*) reminds a Change Agent that it is not the [educational] institution that must change, rather it is the *value system* holding it together that must receive intervention. The educator must first believe that writing in cursive by hand is an element in holistic learning and development.

A study [40] of the approach to teaching handwriting used in France reveals the country's high regard for the skill: "a fundamental physical skill that when mastered, unlocks the mind." Handwriting instruction begins at 3 until age 9. It takes precedence over reading "because writing is more demanding." When writing by hand is automatic, "the children's minds are liberated to release their ideas more efficiently and creatively on paper."

What values does the act of writing in cursive support? Briefly, writing exercises implicitly teach focus on completing tasks, perseverance, respect for order, an appreciation for beauty, consistency, freedom of expression, exploration, and discipline. Dr. Phyllis Rand [4] (Chair of Education, Pensacola Christian College, Florida) refers to Eric Jensen's book, "Teaching with the Brain in Hand" to point out the following skills taught with writing by hand: "prediction, attention, sequencing, estimation, patience, and creativity."

Dr. Vimala Rodgers asserts in her book, "Your Handwriting Can change Your Life" [34], that writing by hand is a character-building tool. "Handwriting... is a diagram of our unconscious mind.... Each movement of the pen not only reflect attitudes about ourselves, [but also] reinforces them."

J. Crebbin [32], not as concerned with letters joining but more with values that each letter feature teaches, presents the Vimala Alphabet as a way for "children to connect to innate spiritual wisdom and express their noblest human traits."[p. 12] She expands on Dr. Rodger's exposition on graphology and how graphotherapy can 'reconfigure neuropathways in the brain that record self-image" [p. 17]. Crebbin uses the following terms to help children in the study and practice of writing cursive letters: <u>zones</u>, where strokes are made and locations are compared to the features of the human body; <u>margins,</u> representing specific concepts of relating to authority, to the past, and the future, as well as to aesthetics; <u>page orientation</u>, which is in the 'landscape direction'; <u>baseline</u>, especially when color-coded, serves as the frame of reference for writing upper and lower case letters within the prescribed zone; <u>slant</u>, revealing one's control over emotions, with the ideal direction leaning towards the right, and with a more upright angle; <u>pressure</u>, which is affected by the pencil grip, indicating one's enthusiasm for life; <u>spacing</u> between words, reflecting one's emotional distance to others.

Drawing the Vimala Alphabet with connecting letters (and standalone lower case g,y,v,s,p,c; k,x, and upper case X) develops writing habits that "reflect thinking habits" [1, 34]. As with Crebbin, Dr. Rodgers reports clients who have reshaped attitudes about self-concept, self-image, and potential by altering their handwriting patterns [p. 24]. Re-shaping one's letter formations re-shapes the mind. For example, the letter c = C teaches complete trust and willingness to be vulnerable; the letter j= J helps to listen to intuition or the voice within; w = W expresses openness to learning and willingness to share knowledge.

In the classroom, Crebbin directs a teacher's attention to the penmanship of a student for gaining insight into the child [p. 21]. Is the child hesitant to raise his hand, hence has low participation in class? Is the child introverted in class? Crebbin would suggest a focused exercise on drawing the letter 'A', for example, knowing that qualities for the drawing 'A' like "sharing what we know", the sound of 'ah" for 'A', and its graphology, a child can be guided on self-assessment: by comparing his letter formation with the model drawings 'A a'.

At the Waldorf School System in North America, correct practice of penmanship in the cursive style of the Vimala Alphabet allows the teacher to literally shape the child's "soul development". Every letter imprints in the child the spiritual quality that the letter embodies. Incredulous as it may seem, the practice of the letter 'K' calmed down a rebellious class—the letter communicated valuing for authority [p 4].

D. Teach Creative Journaling with Cursive

Author Patrick McGee refers to the process of making connections among ideas and of internalizing them a form of 'brain-dance' [36] between the left and the right hemispheres. Brain imaging research has long shown that a variety of areas on <u>both</u> sides of the brain are activated when interpreting metaphors. Literal language, on the other hand, is processed in known language areas in the left hemisphere. In a study [39] on figurative speech, scientists suspect that the "brain triggers related concepts when processing a metaphor's meaning." Journaling in cursive one's reflections on a class topic — using metaphors as a literary device — has proven to be an effective conduit for self-expression. Journaling in cursive would enhance brain activity for creative work.

A proponent of creative journaling by children is Dr. Lucia Cappacione, an Art Therapist with a doctorate in Psychology. Dr. Cappacione proposes that journaling is a "tool for gaining self-understanding and [for] practicing language skills through writing and drawing." [19] When children write, they develop imagination, creative abilities, concentration, clarity, and a positive self-esteem. Cappacione's *Teacher Guide* is a series of exercises that are arranged from simple to complex and from concrete experiences to imaginative visualization, from which the teacher can choose according to what "feels right" for the children in the classroom [p 3]. Journaling could be a culminating activity to process a child's personal meaning of the academic subject.

Interestingly, creative journaling is a method that reflects the CCSS' Language Arts standards for "narrative writing through the grades" with a "command of sequence and detail.... essential for effective argumentative and informative writing." [20]

Although Dr. Capaccione did not suggest the writing mode of text creation, neuroscience studies point towards writing by hand in cursive to be the most beneficial for the development of the executive functions of the brain.

Journaling is a way for metacognition, i.e., reflecting on our own thoughts. Stephen M. Fleming, a cognitive neuroscientist, succinctly writes of studies on 'how the brain analyzes its own computations' [37]. Psychologists now know that metacognition can be trained, with neuroplasticity in brain circuits induced, and the ability to make self-judgments about one's abilities can be improved. Studies in child development show that metacognition, which is an aspect of introspection, is key to educational success.

Fleming cites the findings of educational psychologist Keith Thiede of Boise State University that summarizing a topic with a few words "led to greater metacognitive accuracy" [page 37]. A student, then, would be advised to reallocate study time to least understood material.

While no one has documented neural changes after improvements in metacognition, replicate studies have shown improved memory of word-pairs after a short delay from presentation of those word pairs—much better than if they were asked about them immediately after. A student, then, should be encouraged to "take a break before deciding how well [s/he] has studied for an upcoming test."

A study by Andrea McCrindle and Carol Christensen [46] of 40 first year biology students showed how a group using the journal method of writing their learning processes, compared to the group writing a scientific report, recruited more metacognitive strategies and showed construction of more complex, related, integrated knowledge when learning from text. The journal group performed significantly better in final examinations.

These psychological strategies can be effectively implemented in the classroom of any subject matter, including STEM. Creative journaling can include all aspects of techniques that help students paraphrase what they think they know and reflect on meanings and self-knowledge that surface in the process of introspection.

E. Teach Writing to Heal, in Cursive

When emotional experiences are translated into language, does the act of writing release the individual from trauma's grip? In "The Writing Cure", [35] authors Stephen Lepore and Joshua Smyth present a series of experiments "exploring inhibition, automatic activity, and health." Studies showed a positive correlation between writing about experiences, positive or negative, and absence of or reduction of health problems. They contend that writing forces one to pause and reflect on life. Writing about emotional topics changes cognitive organization, i.e., the way the mind arranges information. Recent studies in cognitive science and neuro-psychology indicate that writing seems to free-up working memory. For students, this meant better grades. [p.286]

Incidentally, Scientific American Mind [38] reports on how expressive writing may facilitate recovery from injury. Writing deepest thoughts and feelings, e.g. journaling, benefits physical health, with reduction in psychological trauma and improvement in mood. Cited as published in the January issue of *Psychosomatic Medicine*, researchers in New Zealand compared the healing progress of two groups who had had biopsies performed on them. Seventy-six percent of the group who engaged in expressive writing showed full healing (and improved sleep) compared with the 42 percent healed among those who did not write.

The New England study, led by Dr. Elizabeth Broadbent of the University of Auckland is supported by the findings of a paper published in the *British Journal of Health Psychology*: writing about an emotional topic lowered participants' cortisol levels.

When long-term emotional upset increase levels of stress hormones (such as cortisol), the immune system is compromised.

Reflective writing in creative journaling allows distancing one's self from an unpleasant experience. Published in 2011 was a collaborative study [50] among psychologists Walter Mischel (then at Stanford University), Angela L. Duckworth (University of Pennsylvania), and Ethan Kross (University of Michigan), demonstrating how reflective writing helped with the process of watching an event unfold from a distance, and place associated emotions in an abstract context. With 110 fifth grade students participating, they found out that those who wrote essays after recalling an experience "dwelled considerably less on the emotional features and included fewer blame statements and more insightful reappraisals" of what happened.

The idea of embodied cognition [35.1] may play a role in hand-writing for healing. The physical act of writing down feelings taps into the unconscious and influences the overt behavior of the writer. For example, a sixth grade teacher instructs a class (or individual) to write about feelings on a traumatic incident as a way to defuse the emotion around the experience. During and after writing, the teacher reports a change in student behavior from anxious to more subdued, preparing them with more focus for the target lesson.

Crebbin [32] and Vimala [34] would enhance the reflective writing process with the use of the Vimala style of cursive writing.

F. Teach K-3 Multi-Lingual Mastery: Manuscript writing, Cursive writing, Keyboarding

Among proponents of teaching how to write by hand, there is debate on which handwriting style should be taught first—print

Teaching Strategies for Penmanship and Legibility

or cursive? What is the place of keyboarding for word processing in developing foundations for literacy and comprehension?

Dr. Virginia Berninger, a professor of educational psychology at the University of Washington is a leading researcher on handwriting development. Her commentary [5] at the National Association of State Boards (NASBE) publication (March 2013) offers an approach for preparing with writing skills the 2027 graduate for twenty-first century work. Dr. Berninger's studies have made a case for teaching both forms of producing text—by hand and by electronic means—timed at developmental learning stages K-3. Here is a summary of the teaching sequence for multilingual mastery of letter production:

Pre K: fine-tip marker/pencils to complete images. Write in manuscript name, alphabet letters, connect dots with arrows to form letters.

K Say the name of and write in manuscript all lower and upper case letters with teacher model letter formation, tracing letters with eyes closed, and writing letters from memory with pencil/marker. Type letters (keyboard) with index finger.

Grade 1 Use both manuscript and keyboarding to practice:

    a) Writing from memory, while naming them, the alphabet in lower case.

    b) Adding capital letters, while naming them

    c) Independently composing letters

Grade 2 a) Same as first grade, but focus on both legibility and automaticity.

    b) Write in manuscript the letter before or after teacher names the letter, which research shows increases composition length across modes.

Grade 3 a) Same as first grade, but teach lower case cursive, showing how connecting strokes links letters alone and in words, with focus on legibility.

Although the teaching sequence of print-to-cursive is challenged by two separate studies [3, 14] it must be noted that in those studies, the switch to cursive occurred in the second grade, not in the third grade as above, with a conclusion that teaching letter grapheme is best in Grade 1 with cursive alone.

These differing conclusions call for more comparative studies at all levels K-12.

G. Teach Cursive Writing with Modified Instruction to Students with Special Needs

How do the Common Core State Standards apply guidelines to students with disabilities? The following are excerpts (bold markings are this author's): "... researched-based instructional and a focus on their effective implementation will help improve **access** to mathematics and English language arts (ELA) standards for **all** students, **including** those with **disabilities**." ... "but **retain** the rigor and **high expectations** of the Common Core State Standards." One can infer that the academic standards are not modified for even "those with most significant cognitive disabilities" because for improved "access", they "may be provided with additional "instructional supports for learning, ... instructional accommodations, ... [and] assistive technology devices and services.."

How these guidelines may be affecting today's Special Education teacher is beyond the scope of this paper's inquiry. However, while debate may be ongoing regarding using the *same* achievement standards for students with special needs, these students are entitled to the same benefits of proper instruction on cursive writing. Unfortunately, according to Dr. Berninger [5], the accommodation afforded those with difficulty with writing by hand [due to poor motor skills] is *keyboarding* on a computer, <u>instead of teaching them *how to write*</u>.

There is a positive correlation between fluency in writing by hand and literacy skills. An action research study for improving practice of teaching was conducted in Middlesex, England by Donna Barratt and Sue Wheatly [40] with 1,192 students ages 11-16 (large secondary comprehensive school) to examine the role of handwriting in raising achievement. They found out that "<u>handwriting speed</u> was a factor in student achievement, regardless of skill", and that those who scored higher than expected in standard examinations had "better handwriting style than those who underachieved". Those in the seventh year of schooling showed a correlation between handwriting speed and reading/spelling.

Slow hand-writers had problems with "poor motor coordination, spelling, letter formation, word shape, and discrimination between upper and lower case." And even those with severe difficulties expressed concern about the appearance of their penmanship.

Dr. Berninger [5] advocates the examination of education policy for a diverse population that includes students with disabilities and students whose native language's writing code is different from English's, as well an acknowledgement by CCSS of the biological limitations of those who struggle with writing because of dysgraphia (affects spelling), dyslexia (impaired word-reading and spelling), and dyscalculia (impaired written calculation).

Conclusions

Feasible Courses of Action

The inquiry on writing by hand and in cursive style was prompted by at least two events: the unexplained exclusion of cursive writing instruction from the Common Core State Standards and by the move of the initial 7 states to keep cursive writing in their curricula: [44] California, Idaho, Indiana, Kansas, Massachusetts, North Carolina, and Utah.

It appears that the act of writing in cursive not only taps into brain activity across regions more than any other present mode of text production; it is also an exercise that strengthens *fluid intelligence*. Just as physical strength can be built with proper nutrition and weight lifting, can intelligence be sharpened with brain exercises? Some research laboratories have seen improvement in IQ scores after brain training "in as little as 3 weeks" [51]. The target is *fluid intelligence*—how one handles tasks, *not* how much facts are known. It is an inherited trait that can be honed for academic and professional achievement through various strategies, e.g. study methods, test-taking approaches, reasoning logic. Most recent study efforts that look at "cognitive training activities" especially those that "exercise working memory" have concluded that the training does not 'expand' working memory, but improves the ability to 'tune out distractions' [51]. <u>Hand-writing thoughts down in cursive is a valuable cognitive training activity that K-12 students should not be deprived of.</u>

There are students with great difficulty maintaining attention span. Without cursive writing, students with special needs face even greater risk of being left behind. "Access" to mathematics and ELA standards begins with *specialized* instructions on how to write. This attention to instruction materials should include those that accommodate students who write with the left hand (10 percent of the world population) and those who are ambivelous (awkward with both hands). Diane Ravitch's [20.1] sharp reproach on high stakes testing for CCSS that has made it worse for the disadvantaged, especially the poor, brings to light multiple benefits of cursive writing skill as a tool for better reading comprehension and composition skills. Better spellers make better readers. Writing fluency, featuring automaticity and speed, allow better note-taking skills and processing of information. Being able to keep up with lectures in class promotes an encouraging learning climate. Learning through writing exercises to be "careful, orderly, neat, clean, responsible, thorough, exacting, and persistent" [4] are characteristics that are required of collaborative work, now and in the future.

A count of publications on the issue of cursive writing reveal more opinions than action research on the effects of cursive writing on academic outcomes. There is a need for more comparative and duplicate studies on the relevance of cursive writing to learning.

To acknowledge the call for more consistent research data from each grade level K-12 requires an acknowledgement of cursive writing's <u>possible value</u> to learning and to development of self-worth. The study needs to happen now, as a longitudinal study would require a generation of graduates for validity and reliability of results. For example, there are conclusions of studies that conflict: teach only one writing style, *but best if cursive only beginning Grade 1*; [3, 4] teach print-keyboard-cursive Grades 1-3 [5].

Let research be longitudinal, national, cross-State, duplicated studies of two sets of K-12 populations, one whose curriculum includes cursive writing for composition and the other straight to keyboarding without requiring the study of cursive. New Zealand, [50] for example, invested in a long-term study on connections between self-control and success in 1,000 children, who were tracked and evaluated for a self-control score by teachers and parents at ages 3-11 on "levels of aggression, hyperactivity, lack of persistence, inattention, and impulsivity." At the participant age of thirty-two years, the 2011 report concluded that those with lower scores "were poorer, had worse health, and more likely to have committed crime than those with more self-control." The resulting determination of appropriate strategies to teach executive function skills during primary and secondary grades then became evidence-based decisions.

Begin the comparative researches *now* on the effects of cursive writing to academic outcomes. When the jury is in about the relevance of cursive writing and of the legibility of penmanship to innovative behavior for creative problem solving, then the Gestalt of CCSS' implementation strategy may be assessed properly.

We have, in the meantime, conclusions of neuroscientists, psychologists, physiologists, occupational therapists, and remedial reading specialists that help the educator piece together the relationships of the hand and the brain. We have social scientists, economists, and visionaries who project trends in the nature of work and the skills required by future organizations. While we wait for proof that writing by hand *may* be irrelevant to creativity and innovation, <u>why not work on the studied benefits of cursive writing</u>? Adding keyboarding skills is an answer to future needs of digital communication, but its operational features <u>do not</u> replace those of penning thoughts on paper.

I propose for the system of Education to pay heed *now* to multidisciplinary findings on the relationship of hand activity, writing by hand, brain development, and innovation, all of which seem to point towards the wisdom of reinstalling the study of 'penmanship'. For today's curriculum, include keyboarding for word processing, and <u>only after</u> producing writing outlines and a first draft by hand. Teach cursive as an art of forming letters, and create the positively joyous learning climate using movement and music. Employ journaling for expressive writing on thoughts and personal meaning about a lesson. Consider E.A. Enstrom's suggestion to double—grade handwritten work to encourage students: one for content, one for quality of penmanship [8]. However, follow L. Cappacione's (19) reminder <u>not</u> to attach journaling to grades and judgment.

To reinstall cursive writing in the classroom is to reinstall the memes for it. Unless the policy makers in the educational system and its teachers *believe* that legibility in penmanship is important, that cursive writing is a creative preoccupation, that one's handwriting is self-evident, and that it incites the brain to keep firing synapses for knowing, then the visionaries' picture of Tomorrow may be *lacking* in participants who are able to respond to its requirements for a life with meaning.

Feasible Courses of Action

The inclusion of cursive writing in today's curricula adds to efforts for holistic education. Learning legible penmanship in cursive style joins the resurgence of interest in traditional learning activities such as drills in facts and memorization of the multiplication table. The wonderment of automation in the digital age has distorted the value of the memoriter approach to learning and the need to slow down for reflection with meditative hand-writing.

Indeed, a closer examination of the CCSS's reading and strands for English Language Arts justify giving instructions on cursive writing, for how else can you better develop skills required to "read deeply and wide[ly]"? Initial studies show that keyboarding does not trigger brain activity that text production by hand does. Writing by hand in cursive must be taught in schools and at home, now, in preparation for twenty-first century work and living. Opportunities for classroom encouragement on quality work in cursive abound in all subjects; for example, labeling maps by hand in Geography, written conclusions in a Mathematics problem, describing feelings about a classmate's art project or a character in a story, identifying common ground and differences among publications.

To teach cursive writing, however, is <u>to know how to teach it correctly</u>. Director of Research and Instruction Dr. E.A Enstrom's lamentation on the "sad state of pupil's handwriting" was published in two essays, with the second calling for teachers to have access to "both pre-service and in-service education" in sound handwriting skills, so that they may provide "students with numerous good examples in their own chalkboard work or handwritten comments." [8] A superintendent was quoted to have said that a teacher's board work is reflected in the student's penmanship. Called *incidental learning*, the teacher's penmanship on the board influences what the students learn in letter formation. What Dr. Enstrom emphasized cannot be paraphrased better: "to fortify these [handwriting] skills in the classroom, teachers should insist upon high standards for all handwritten assignments and motivate students to achieve an efficient, rapid script by rewarding legible work, by keeping files of student handwriting samples to check progress...." These guidelines sound right on target for achieving CCSS standards, don't they? *They were written in 1961 and 1966.*

The political issue of teacher training on cursive writing was briefly noted by the Indiana University report on Dr. James' study [2]. It asked the question on whether or not teacher training was an issue of overhead cost to CCSS implementation, "hence" its probable exclusion of cursive writing in the standards.

On another note, when Betty Edwards [28] and Jennifer Crebbin [32] ask seminar participants who would wish that their penmanship were better, hands shoot up in the air. A sustained valuing through the twelfth grade for legible and neat writing in cursive would eliminate the common self-reproach and apologies for having 'bad' penmanship. Incidentally, the Associated Press [44] ends its article on handwriting with a word of caution for adults who are unable to write in cursive. It tells of President Obama joking that Treasury Secretary, Jacob Lew, needed to practice his signature [a series of loops] before affixing it to the US currency *"to make at least one letter legible in order not to debase our currency."*

A last word on writing by hand brings us back to the beginnings of writing. Alfred Fairbank's "The Story of Handwriting" [41] captures this best: Language and speech make it possible to share stories and keep records [p.20]: "what is valued in the correspondence of our friends is the inevitable expression of personality [p.18]. Writing allows us to "know something of the life of people even after the lapse of thousands of years" [p.17]. In this age of message transmission by a mere thumb on a key, I cannot imagine <u>not knowing</u> what the handwriting of a friend or of one's ancestor looks like and claim that I *know* him as a person. Neither can I imagine future generations being able to truly appreciate with full comprehension a historical document like the *Declaration of Independence* that has been *re-typed* in Helvetica font because no one can read the original in cursive, and totally miss the pleasure of seeing the original written in the penmanship of the author.

If visionaries like Ken Robinson [10], David Peat [29], Tony Wagner [23], Linda Hill [24], Howard Gardner [9], Daniel Pink [21], Douglas Thomas [22], and John Seeley Brown [22] are certain about the future skills and aptitudes for innovative thinking that are required of the twenty-first century labor force, then the Board of Education may have cause to worry about the readiness of a generation. If we cease to write by hand and rely on keyboarding for record-keeping, what happens when the power grid fails and all lights are out? Where would society find the well of wisdom from which to draw creative and critical thinking? Would we have the traits of resilience, organization, patience, self-regulation, and empathy called for in a survival mode? Would we have developed the executive functions of the brain through which these traits are exercised?

In a material world where things of consequence are measured by numbers, it is very easy to lose sight of the links among self-fulfillment, introspection, meaning, and happiness. Writing opens the window to the soul; without words and fluency to write them how can there be expression? The motion of hand-writing taps into the creative workings of the brain. With cursive writing, the academic environment could be the stage that fosters Martin Seligman's elements of authentic happiness: positive emotion, engagement, relationship, meaning, and accomplishment.

Oral and written stories mark the passage of time in human history. The soul of the story, however, is in the stroke of the hand that carved it. And *that* ability to capture the story's soul, in the end, is what we could lose without using our hands to pen our thoughts, or join someone's journey when following his quill.

Post script:

A silver lining behind the technological cloud is in the horizon for writing by hand with a mode for audio retrieval. Already we see two ball point pens for hand-written note-taking that record audio as text is written, with the option of sending files of notes to cloud storage. Interview data for this paper was noted by hand using *livescribe*^{tm}. When I wrote notes during an interview, I remembered how I wrote the content; *livescribe*^{tm} allowed me to hear once again the emotional content of the text as it was evoked.

This paper was initially composed by hand in cursive style using lined paper and blue gel ink. The first draft was then typed in MS Word and printed on paper for manual editing with a retractable pencil. File storage was executed with back-up, in deathly fear of losing the document during a sudden power outage.

—cmbatan 3-18-2015

Works Cited

1. Miller, Samuel. Teaching Handwriting Helps Students Achieve. *Information for Educators. McGraw-Hill Education.*

2. James, Karin Harman. Printing, Cursive, Keyboarding: What's The Difference When It Comes to Learning? *Retrieved from http.newsinfoiu.edu/news-archive/20977.html. January 2, 2012.*

3. Montesinos-Gelet. Learning Cursive in the First Grade Helps Students. *Universite de Montreal.* Released September 16, 2013.

4. Rand, Phyllis. The Benefits Of Teaching Cursive First. *A BEKA Book Review.* Retrieved February 2015.

5. Berninger, Virginia. Educating Students in the Computer Age to Be Multilingual By Hand. *Commentaries, National Association of State Boards of Education (NASBE).* March 2013.

6   Wikipedia. English Cursive in the US. Retrieved March 15, 2015. TEACHER TRAINING. Also footnote 40

7   Supon, Vi. Cursive Writing: Are Its Last Days Approaching? *Journal of Instructional Psychology,* Vol. 36, No. 4. Pages 357-359. Footnote for LINGUISTIC DIVERSITY

8   Enstrom, E.A. (1966, January) HANDWRITING: THE Neglect of a Needed Skill. *The Clearing House, v40 n5.* Pages 308-310.

9   Gardner, Howard. (2008) *5 Minds for the Future.* MA: Harvard Business Press.

10 Robinson, Ken. (2001). *Out Of Our Minds. Learning To Be Creative.* Rev. 2011. UK: Capstone Publishing Ltd.

11 Csikszentmihalyi, Mihaly. (1990). *FLOW.* USA: Harper & Row.

12 Kersey, Alyssa & James, Karin H. (2013, September 23). Brain Activation patterns resulting from learning letter forms through active self-production and passive observation in young children. *Cognitive Science. Frontiers in Psychology, doi:10.3389/fpsyg.2013.00567.*

13 Wilson, Frank R. (1998). *The Hand. How Its Use Sharpen The Brain, Language, and Human Culture.* New York: Vintage Books.

13.1 Seiffer, Marc J. (October 1, 2002. The Telltale Hand: How Writing Reveals The Damaged Brain. *The Dana Foundation.*

14 Morin, Marie-France, Lavoie, Natalie, & Montesinos, Isabelle. (2012) The Effects of Manuscript, Cursive or Manuscript/Cursive Styles on Writing Development in Grade 2. *Language Literacy, Volume 4, Issue 1.*

Works Cited

15   Keim, Brandon. (2013, September/October). The Science of Handwriting. *Scientific American Mind.* Pages 54-59.

16   Jabr, Ferris. (2013, November). Why the Brain Prefers Paper. *Scientific American.* Pages 50-53.

17   Hardiman, Mariale. Why NeuroEducation Matters—How the Science of Learning Influences Educational Practices. *Video of keynote speech. Downloaded February 2015.*

18   Hardiman, Mariale. (2012, April 12) Brain-Targetted Teaching Model. *TEDxEnola video of presentation.*

19   Capacchione, Lucia. (1989). The *Creative Journal for Children. A guide for Parents, Teachers, and Counselors.* Boston & London, Shambala.

20   The Common Core State Standards. www.commoncore.org. Retrieved February 22, 2015.

20.1   Strauss, Valerie. Speech by Diane Ravitch to the Modern Language Association on January 11, 2014. Online copy forwarded by J. Trifone, MALT 15-03, TGI, 2014.

21   Pink, Daniel. (2006). *A Whole New Mind. Why the Right-Brainer Will Rule The Future.* NY: Riverhead Books.

22   Thomas, Douglas & Brown, John Seeley. (2011). *A New Culture of Learning. Cultivating the Imagination for A World of Constant Change.* SC: (Brown & Seeley)

23   Wagner, Tony. Play, Passion, Purpose. TEDxNYED video presentation. Viewed March 2015.

24   Cook, Gareth. (2015, March/April. *Scientific American*). All Together Now. An interview with Professor Linda Hill of Harvard Business School on how to unleash an organization's collective genius and innovation.

25   Wikipedia. SHODO. Retrieved March 2015.

25.1 EIDO TAI SHIMANO. (1992) *Zen Word Zen Calligraphy.* Boston & London: Shambala.

25.2 YUJIRO NAKATA. (1983) *The Art of Japanese Calligraphy.* New York/Tokyo: Weatherhill/Heibonshu.

26   Wikipedia. SAT. Retrieved February 2015.

27   Buzan, Tony. (1996). *The Mind Map Book.* New York: The Penguin Book. Pages 48-49, 89-90.

28   Edwards, Betty (1989). *Drawing on The Right Side of the Brain. A Course in Enhancing Creativity and Artistic Confidence.* Revised Edition. New York: Penguin Putnam Inc.

29   Peat, David F. (2000). *The Blackwinged Night. Creativity in Nature and Mind.* MA: Perseus Publishing.

30   Eisner, Elliot W. (2002) The *Arts and the Creation of Mind.* New Haven & London: Yale University Press.

31   Hensher, Philip. (2012). *The Missing Ink. The Lost Art of Handwriting.* New York: Farber and Farber.

32   Crebbin, Jennifer. (2007). *Soul Development through Handwriting.* MA: Steiner Books.

33   Wikipedia. Rudolf Steiner's Eurythm. Retrieved February 2015.

34   Rodgers, Vimala. (2000). *Your Handwriting Can Change Your Life.* New York: Simon & Schuster.

Works Cited

35   Lepore, Stephen J. & Smyth, Joshua M. (2002). *The Writing Cure. How Expressive Writing Promotes Health and Emotional Well-Being.* US: American Psychological Association. Page 286.

35.1 Bargh, John A. (2014, January). Our Unconscious Mind. *Scientific American.* Page 34.

36   McGee, Patrick T. (Rev 1998). *Brain Dancing. Work smarter, Learn Faster, and Manage Information More Efficiently.* Bellevue, Washington: Braindance.com Inc.

37   Fleming, Stephen M. (2014, September/October). The Power of Reflection. *Scientific American Mind.* Pages 31-37.

38   Rodriguez, Tori. (2013, November/December). Write to Heal. *Scientific American Mind.* Page 17.

39   Rodriguez, Tori. (2013, November/December). Figurative speech Sways Decisions. *Scientific American Mind.* Cited from PLOS ONE, January.

40   Barratt, Donna & Wheatly, Sue. (1997) Case Study 2: The Role of Handwriting in Raising Achievement. (An Action Research). Report, Teacher Training Agency. Excerpted from book by Kashy, Valan (2005). *Action Research for Improving Practice. A Practical Guide.* London: Paul Chapman Publishing/ A SAGE Publishing Company.

41   Fairbank, Alfred. (1970) *The Story of Handwriting. Origins and Development.* New York: Watson-Guptill Publications.

42   Mueller, Pam A. & Oppenheimer, Daniel M, (2014, June). The Pen is Mightier Than the Keyboard. Advantages of Longhand Over Laptop Note Taking. *Psychological Science.* Vol. 25 no. 6 1159-1168.

43   Thompson, William Forde & Schlaug, Gottfried. (2015, March/April). The Healing Power of Music. *Scientific American Mind.* Pages 34-39.

44   The Associated Press. (2013, November 15). States Fight To Keep Cursive Handwriting in the Classroom. Downloaded January 2015.

45   Posted online geralyndeyproject (2014, May 1) 6 Reasons to Reject the Common Core State Standards for K-Grade 3. Retrieved May 2014.

46   McCrindle, Anrea R. & Christensen, Carol A. The Impact of Learning journals on Metacognitive and Cognitive Processes and Learning Performance. ScienceDirect.com (through UCONN Libraries). Retrieved March 2015.

47   Bosse, Marie-Line, Chaves, Natalie, & Valdois, Sylviane. (2014, February 10). Lexical orthography acquisition: Is handwriting better than spelling aloud? *Frontiers in Psychology.* Doi:10.3389/fpsyg.2014.00056.

48   Posted online McKenzie, Betsy. Handwriting Improves Memory Retention. *Out of the Jungle.* Quoted by researchers in the *Science Daily Report's* interview with Professor Mangen and on book, "Advances in Haptics". Retrieved May 25, 2014.

49   Ouellette, Gene & Tims, Talisa. (2014, February 13). The write way to spell: printing vs. typing effects on orthographic learning, Frontiers *in Psychology.* Doi:10.3389/fpsyg.2014.00117.

50   Wickelgren, Ingrid. (2012, September/October). The Education of Character. *Scientific American Mind.* Pages 46-58.

51   Jonides, John, Jaeggi, Susanne M, & Buschkuehl, Martin. (2013, September/October). Building Better Brains. *Scientific American Mind*. Pages 59-63.

Appendix A

SAMPLES OF PENMANSHIP
K-12 and Adult Education

<u>Grades 1-9, northern Philippines, where English is a 2nd language and the medium of instruction</u>

Grade 1   age: 1
(F)   I am writing in Print.

(M) - 7 I am writing in Print.

Grade 2   age 7
(F)   i'm writing in cursive

(M)   i'm writing in   age 8
      cursive

Grade 3   age 9
(F)   I am writing in cursive

                                                    age 9
(M)   I am writing in cursive.

Appendix A

Grades 1-9, northern Philippines, where English is a 2nd language and the medium of instruction

Grade 4 — Age: 10
(M) - I am writing in cursive.

(F) - I am writing in cursive. — age: 10

Grade 5 — Age: 12
(M) - I am writing in cursive.

(F) - I am writing in cursive. — age: 11

(F) Age: 12 — Grade 6
I am writing in cursive.

(M) 12
I am writing in cursive.

Middle School in Stamford CT

Grade 6

Please write your answer below.

Student Name: _____

ms tori should let my brother in he is in 3rd grade and wants to know what middle school is like.

my brothers name is Evan, all the things he can see in elementry school kids like to walk the halls but in Dolan Middle school if your on the first floor and you have to go to the 3rd floor you'll have to walk up the stairs and you never get used to the it like someone is hunching you right in the legs why your almost at the top.

but lunch in dolan middle school lunch is fun omi lishis you'll Realy like it Evan.

Appendix A

Middle School in Stamford CT

Student Name:

Grade 6

Please write your answer below.

Student Name: _____

Have you ever dreamed of inviting some to your school? Well I would invite one of my faivorite soccer players Lionel Messi. He is really amazing because he is a soccer player, cancer suvivor, and childhood

One reason Lionel Messi should come to this school is because he is a soccer player. Lionel Messi kicks like lightning speed bolt and a chettah. This soccer player is also very good at making a lot of goals for his team. Messi plays for Argentina and Barcelona. Lionel Messi is really a good inspiration. Maybe, once he can teach some kids at Dolan to play soccer.

Another reason Lionel Messi should visit Dolan is because he is a cancer survivor. Once Lionel Messi was about to grow a 6th finger in his hand. People were really scared that they tremmbled in fear when people saw

Spelling practice →

Grade 5, Elementary School in Stamford CT
(privately tutored)

saxophone — Being a member of the band is enjoyable for me. I like to play
saxophone — the ~~saxophone~~ with the other musical
instruments — ~~enstrooments~~ use make ~~beautiful~~ *& beautiful*
occasion — music. ~~&~~ We enjoy ~~to~~ practicing after school. On (speical) ~~ocasions~~ *occasion*
special — ~~ttith~~ With all ~~thes~~ these ~~activityies~~ *activities* *special*
I enjoy my friends in the band.
When I grow ~~op~~ up I will remember our
S B — ~~tember~~ Springdale band.
↑
teacher's notes

B   B   B

Appendix A

Grades 1-9, northern Philippines, where English is a 2nd language and the medium of instruction

Grade 7 — Age: 13
(M) I am writing in cursive
(F) I am writing in cursive — Age: 13

Grade 8 — Age: 13
(M) I am writing in cursive
(F) I am writing in cursive — Age: 13

Grade 9 — Age: 15
(M) I am writing in cursive
(F) I am writing in cursive — Age: 15

Norwalk middle school, 8th grade, privately tutored on cursive writing

Cursive writing is important to me. It keeps me focus on what I am writing, not only on ideas but also on spelling and letter formation. Cursive writing is a good mental activity to do over the summer when most activities are physical. To be able to write in cursive is an accomplishment for me.

Ryan Link   8th grade
August 17, 2016   Norwalk, CT

Grade 12 in Norwalk CT

5.

pg 146 # 23-26

23. Weight is the gravitational force acting on an object. Mass is the amount of matter in an object.

24. $m = .150$ kg   a. $F_{net} = -mg$
 $v_i = 20$ m/s $= -(.150 \text{ kg})(9.81 \text{ m/s}^2)$
 $g = 9.81$ m/s² $= \boxed{-1.47\text{N}}$
      b. $\boxed{-1.47\text{N}}$

25a.   b.

   c.   d.

26. $m = 5.5$ kg   a. $F_n = mg = (5.5 \text{ kg})(9.81 \text{ m/s}^2)$
 $g = 9.8$ m/s² $= \boxed{54\text{N}}$
 $\theta = 12°$ b. $F_n = mg(\cos\theta) = (5.5)(9.81)(\cos 12°)$
 $\theta = 25°$ $= \boxed{53\text{N}}$
 $\theta = 45°$ c. $F_n = mg(\cos\theta) = (5.5)(9.81)(\cos 25°)$
                              $= \boxed{49\text{N}}$

Language Arts Teacher, northern Philippines

Misplaced Adjectives (Gehraer)

1. She has a friend with a dimple named Susan.

2. The rice wrapper was taken from the freezer and given to the chef stiff as a board.

3. The pork chops were tempting to the boys sizzling on the broiler.

4. Yoko Ono talked about her husband, John Lennon, who was killed in an interview with Barbara Walters.

5. A calf was born to a farmer with two tails.

6. Some reports said shortly after his death Mao Tse Tung had expressed a wish that his body be cremated.

Appendix A

Adult Education, schooled in Russia

2) When dealing with difficult individuals it is important to stay calm and listen to what they have to say. When people come at you with complaints and a lot of emotion you need to try and control the conversation. Listen to what they say and try to accommodate them the best you can. Many people during these situations will not calm down until they are venting their problems. Once they are finished you will be able to speak to them and they might have more of a clear mind to understand the situation.

When the customer is upset you need to ask a question to clarify
(What is the best way to reach you? and then confirm)
I am so sorry. How may I help you?

Adult ESL, Bilingual Chinese

1. Driving too fast is dangerous.

   Bungee jumping is dangerous.

2. The Lo-mein is delicious.

   The tea is delicious.

3. The student is studious.

   The boy is studious.

Adult
ESL Chinese Character to English

Appendix A

Adult Education, schooled in Haiti

Lov: "If there anything else I may you help with?

Cust: No, thanks.

Lov: Did I answer all your questions?

Cust: thank you everything is fine. I really appreciate it.

Lov: It's a pleasure. Thank you and have a nice day!

Professional writer in a Community College business course

Open
- It is said that — a fact — 44%
  ~~the most common fear of Americans~~
  is fear public speaking, to put that into perspective
  only 11% of Americans are afraid of dying. As Jerry
  Seinfeld said, people are dying just so they don't
  have to give a eulogy at their own funeral.

Intro Becoming a Toastmaster is the beginning of a quest for
knowledge that will enrich your life
  - Personal story
    - didn't know what I was volunteering for at first
    - led to meeting new colleagues
    - formed new relationships in the Stamford business community

Middle The Importance of Knowledge
The best knowledge is free
  ↳ Altadyne in water
    - libraries
    - The invention of the internet → Inventor vs. Bill
        Mark Zuckerberg
  - Toastmasters $6 a month
    ↳ practice leadership, public speaking

Appendix A

Adult Education, with anxiety disorder

Dear proffesor,

I have real anxiety issues, and panic at times, I + overwhelmed at times, which makes my shake at times, which makes my writing more out of papers. It's hard for me to speak loud due to discomfort in my voice. The shades/sunglasses help intensity

Thanks,

EX: I have a pretty big memory problem, and have to look at notes and study for hours and hours at end end, all day if needed, and usually happens, when studying for the course, dedicate my studies, number one.

Appendix B

List of Elementary School Teachers' Ideas
Workshop Output

"Professional Development Teachers Choice", August 29, 2017. Stamford Public Schools, Stamford, Connecticut, U. S. A.

HOW CURSIVE WRITING COULD BE INCORPORATED
IN DAILY CLASSROOM ACTIVITIES

HOW CURSIVE WRITING COULD BE INCORPORATED IN DAILY CLASSROOM ACTIVITIES.

(Check marks are votes of feasibility from participants)

Morning Group	**Afternoon Group**
Elementary reading:	
✓✓✓✓✓ "dancing out" the letters	
✓✓✓ Identifying letters in nature	
Exit slips	
✓✓ Letter formation to address behavior (*Vimala Alphabet system*)	
Mind Maps	

K	**K / 1st grade**
Morning journals	✓✓✓✓ Alphabet
✓✓✓ weekend news	✓✓✓ Letter of the Week
Red words	colors and shapes
✓✓✓✓ O.G.	✓✓✓ Play doh (letter formation)
✓✓ shaving cream	✓✓✓ shaving cream
✓✓ tracing screens	tracing over mesh screen
✓✓✓ writing their names	✓✓✓ sidewalk chalk
✓✓✓✓ sight words	✓ sky writing (with music)
	✓✓ sand tracing

2ⁿᵈ/3ʳᵈ grade	2ⁿᵈ grade
Name writing	✓word study
Date	✓sight words
Story writing/journaling	✓✓vocabulary
Taking notes	✓morning word work
✓Vocabulary	✓handwriting
✓Phonics	
Morning work	

3ʳᵈ/4ᵗʰ grade

✓✓Mind Map of concepts/facts/ideas related to the figure (in cursive)

✓✓✓✓2-column notes for poster project

Encouraging students to use "first person" when writing about or role-playing character

✓Journaling by other students as they are listening to other role-players

Journaling in first person as character

3ʳᵈ/4ᵗʰ grade	3ʳᵈ grade
	✓✓Reader's Response
✓word work (daily 5)	✓Note taking
✓✓journal entries (daily 5)	✓✓✓social studies
Science	✓✓✓Post Office
✓✓problem solving (math)	✓✓Homework

Appendix B

✓✓✓✓✓O.T. (Handwriting Practice) ✓✓✓✓✓✓cursive writing: quiet activity at end of day

Speech lessons

4th/5th grade | 4th/5th grade

✓Rough drafts
✓✓Note taking
Summarizing
✓✓Vocabulary practice
✓✓Response to reading
✓✓Journaling
✓Answering questions

✓✓✓journal writing
✓✓✓note taking
✓✓✓graphic organizers
formulas (math/science)
✓morning message/morning work
✓✓✓Flash cards
✓✓vocabulary
✓word problems
✓✓daily five rotation (practice skills)
✓bullet-point facts (social studies
Paragraph responses

5th grade

✓✓Draft essay in cursive (Advanced)

✓✓Write in cursive a quote that encapsulates the character of the famous revolutionary hero)

✓✓✓✓draw a picture of the hero and in cursive write the signature

(no grade specified)
✓ Name writing
✓ New Vocabulary
✓ spelling patterns
✓ Word families
✓ Date
Directional words
Movement breaks
✓ Syllabic (multi)
Taking notes

(no grade specified)
Morning meeting
Response to text
✓ feelings journal
✓✓✓ sign in, lunch court, bathroom pass
✓ math problem solving, science
✓ notes, observations
academic choice
✓ writing name, date
✓✓ address, birthday
✓✓ sight words
✓✓ vocabulary
✓ answer on white boards
✓ labeling diagrams
✓ sand writing

-end of list-

Appendix C

KEYBOARDING WITHOUT LEARNING WRITING BY HAND: Issues For The Educator's Consideration

KEYBOARDING WITHOUT LEARNING WRITING BY HAND: Issues For The Educator's Consideration*

"... we teachers are confronted with intriguing evolutions in **technology**. So we pose these questions:

- With electronic data base searches and electronic production of letter shapes, **how do personal computers** affect the young child's study skills for reading and comprehension?

- How do automated functions with a keyboard and screen affect **brain region development for creative and critical thinking**?

- What happens to the process of **recognizing patterns and structures** when the computer does it for the child?

- With finger tap on Google search, how does a child learn **discrete skills involved in locating information**?

- Instead of reading a paper book, how does watching text on screen translate to expressing ideas with **fluidity in evolving metaphors**?

- Could effortless retrieval from cloud storage **establish basic patterns of thought for predicting outcomes**?

- And what influence does technology have on **value systems** that define a child's assumptions about working with others?"

—*Celia M. Batan, BA MA CPC*

*Excerpt from Ms. Batan's Commencement Speech, Masters in Learning & Thinking, The Graduate Institute, Bethany CT. August 8, 2015.

About the Author

Celia M. Batan, BA MA CPC

Celia M. Batan considers herself fortunate in carrying yearly course loads in a variety of fields. She believes that each classroom is an integral part of her role as *educator* who assists students in carving out the story of a course syllabus, knowing that the story is *theirs*, not the teacher's.

Ms. Batan's undergraduate degree is in Social Sciences, majoring in Psychology, from the University of the Philippines. Her graduate degree is in Learning and Thinking from The Graduate Institute in Bethany, CT. She also holds a Certificate in Training & Development from New York University. Ms. Batan is certified to teach adult programs in the State of Connecticut and holds TESOL certifications to teach ESL and TESOL Business English.

Every year Ms. Batan enjoys several teaching positions in counties of Fairfield and New Haven, Connecticut:

Instructor, YALE English Language Institute Summer University Preparation Program for international high school students.

Adjunct Instructor, Extended Studies and Workforce Education Division, Norwalk Community College. Customer Service for Health Care Professionals, Retail Service/Selling Skills, Business Writing, Job Interviewing, Effective Communication and Conversation Skills, Study Skills.

ESL Advisor and *Instructor*, Building1Community (immigrant center). Instructional design and program evaluation: Conversational English for all levels of proficiency, Functional English for vocational service programs.

Assistant Instructor, Aikido Martial Arts, University of Connecticut Stamford; Kids' class, Aikido of Fairfield County

Music Instructor, Convent for an order of nuns. Liturgical and Sacred Music.

Ms. Batan's professional background is in instructional design of skills training programs, initially for Philippine language development of foreign speakers, then for manpower skills and organizational change for Bureau offices of the Philippine government. In the U.S., she designed for publication and distribution custom business communication skills training programs for clients of Exxon, Xerox, and Times Mirror.

Ms. Batan served with the US Peace Corps as a language and culture instructor, designing instruction programs for two major Philippine languages.

Her contributions to the business communities of Fairfield, CT and Westchester, NY have come in varied forms: she is certified to qualify and place job applicants for corporate positions, as well as to conduct public workshops on selling strategies, professional business image, and personal development.

Ms. Batan's background in Martial arts includes practice in Japanese Aikido (Nidan), Iaido (3rd Kyu), Karate (green belt), Judo, the Philippine martial art of stick fighting (arnis/escrima), and the art of Japanese floral arrangements (Ikebana, not ranked).

Ms. Batan's community service includes volunteering for various programs in the City of Stamford: assisting Stamford Public School's Board of Education on reinstatement of cursive writing in the primary grades, teaching at Dolan Middle School's annual Diversity Program, teaching foreign speakers English literacy (beginning reading for adults) at Building1Community, welcoming patrons for Palace Theatre shows, and High Mass choir singing at the Basilica of St. John the Evangelist in Stamford.

Each year it is with pleasure that Ms. Batan looks forward to evolving teaching methods for each of her course assignments, integrating study skills of note-taking with basic brain-mapping techniques in the mode of cursive writing.

cmbatan@hotmail.com

About Dr. James Trifone

Jim Trifone holds a PhD in Education from the University Of Lancaster, UK and has authored numerous publications as well as conducted workshop presentations at universities and National Conferences on concept mapping, motivation, constructivist teaching pedagogies in the United States and abroad. Dr. Trifone brings more than forty years of classroom instruction as a public high school educator and twenty years of educational management to the Master of Arts in Learning and Thinking (MALT) degree program offered at The Graduate Institute in Bethany, Connecticut. As the Academic Director for the MALT degree program, he is responsible for creating and coordinating learning experiences that integrate the content and perspectives of the humanities, arts and the sciences. His passion lies in creating constructivist-learning experiences, which encourage his K-12 teachers to embrace the notion that learning itself is the mechanism of social and personal change in society.

Over the years, Dr. Trifone's various publications have focused on learning strategies that foster students' level of conceptual change learning, as well as motivation to learn. His doctoral dissertation revealed that one strategy for fostering conceptual change learning-*concept mapping*- is not only effective in enhancing students' ability to develop a more meaningful and deeper conceptual understanding, but also a means to motivate students' in becoming self-regulated learners. One of his major instructional goals is to encourage students to become capable, competent and motivated learners who are self-regulated learners. His passion lies in discovering strategies that effectively foster students' active participation in their own learning processes for the expressed purpose of developing a conceptual understanding.

Dr. Trifone's extensive teaching experience and research studies have grounded him in adopting a "systems" approach to learning, knowing, thinking, and teaching, which was central to creating and developing the MALT degree program. Towards this end, he views the role of "teacher" as one responsible in fostering students' development of concepts and skills through active participation in constructing what they learn. Moreover, this perspective views "learner" and "teacher" as co-creators in the participatory framework of learning. Meaningful learning and thinking consists of applying cognitive and metacognitive learning strategies to hands-on and minds-on experiences that challenge preconceived assumptions and level of conceptual understanding.

In summary, as an educator, Dr. Trifone strives to contextualize learning by encouraging students to see and make connections, thus integrating learning in one area with that in another. This framework fosters the acquisition of higher reasoning, as well as critical and creative thinking abilities. From this new perspective, the learner is not perceived as someone disconnected from the learning environment. Rather, the learner is a participatory member of a learning system comprised of the teacher, students and physical learning environment in which they are embedded.

jtrifone@me.com

Acknowledgements

I would not have been able to complete this work with as much joy as I did without the background cheering and willingness of the following to see it through delivery:

Juliana R. Medina, M. Ed., Remedial Reading Elementary, Brent School, Philippines; Family Literacy and ESL Instructor, Stamford CT

Jim Trifone, PhD, Academic Director for Masters in Learning & Thinking Program, The Graduate Institute, Bethany CT

Natalie Elder, M. Ed, Director of School Improvement and Professional Development;
Lisa Armstrong, PhD, Curriculum Associate
for Elementary Literacy. Board of Education,
Stamford Public Schools, Stamford CT

2017 Professional Development attendees:
K-5 Teachers Stamford Public Schools, Stamford CT

Charmaine Tourse, Principal, Dolan Middle School, Stamford CT. Sixth-Seventh grade Language Arts Teachers Nancy Bonardi and Maureen Morrissey; Special Literacy Specialist Kristen Corbi-Miller

Barbara Elena M. Lagos, PhD, Teaching Reading & Language for Preschool Level, St. Louis University, Philippines

Clara Juncadella Otto, M. Ed., Unified Arts/ World Language Instructor for elementary grades, Hartford and New Haven Counties, CT

K-12 teachers in 2013-15 Cohorts for Masters in Learning & Thinking Program, The Graduate Institute in Bethany and Hartford, CT

Robin Moore, MA Writing and Oral Traditions and Faculty, The Graduate Institute, Bethany CT

Sue Greene, President, SGS Personnel, South Salem NY

Parents, teachers, and administrators who were willing to stop and answer survey questions in parking lots, work stations, and grocery aisles

Gene, Karesia, Omi

Global friends, you know who you are.

I thank you all.